"Something happens when women pray. Transformation happens as these African American sisters pray. *Blessed Is She* is a significant book for your journey. These writers have wrapped their femininity in His divinity, and they remind us that transformation matters."

— AMBASSADOR SUZAN JOHNSON COOK, ordained minister; US Ambassador for International Religious Freedom, the Obama Administration; author of *Sister to Sister: Devotions for and from African American Women* and *The Sister's Guide to Survive and Thrive in Ministry*

"This is a brave and bountiful collection of prayer stories, each one drawing us, as women, closer and deeper into the comforting embrace of our loving Father. Our life journeys are complicated, indeed. But when we turn everything over to the One who made and keeps us, then blessed are we. Triumphant and transforming."

— PATRICIA RAYBON, regular contributor to *Our Daily Bread* and (in)courage; board member of Denver Seminary; award-winning journalist and author of *I Told the Mountain to Move: Learning to Pray So Things Change* and *My First White Friend: Confessions on Race, Love, and Forgiveness*

Blessed Is She

THE TRANSFORMING PRAYER JOURNEYS OF

30 AFRICAN AMERICAN WOMEN

VICTORIA SAUNDERS MCAFEE

AND CONTRIBUTORS

Blessed Is She: *The Transforming Prayer Journeys of 30 African American Women*

Interior design by Glynese Northam
Author photo used by permission of The Birth Lens, LLC

Library of Congress Cataloging-in-Publication Data

Names: Saunders McAfee, Victoria, compiler.
Title: Blessed is she : the transforming prayer journeys of 30 African
   American women / Victoria Saunders McAfee and contributors .
Description: Grand Rapids : Discovery House, 2019. | Summary: "Be
   encouraged to intercede for others as you read the prayer stories from
   30 African American women. Discover the joy and strength in partnering
   with God through prayer to impact the lives of others"-- Provided by
   publisher.
Identifiers: LCCN 2019022673 | ISBN 9781627079631 (paperback)
Subjects: LCSH: African American women--Religious life. |
   Prayer--Christianity.
Classification: LCC BR563.N4 B578 2019 | DDC 248.3/2082--dc23
LC record available at https://lccn.loc.gov/2019022673

Printed in the United States of America
20 21 22 23 24 25 26 / 8 7 6 5 4 3

I lovingly dedicate this book to my friend Mary Hinton, who knows my whole story and still is excited about what God has done and will do in and through me.

And to my husband, David McAfee, who is my personal walking Bible commentary and my eye candy all at the same time.

A Simple Prayer for Us

Lord, please transform our prayers for ourselves, our communities, and your world. And thank you for upholding us as you call the lost and lonely into your arms.

Contents

Blessed to Join Intercession

HIDDEN IN HIM—SANDRA FOSTER—125

Blessed After Amen

NO LONGER BOUND—CURTIS ANDRE JOHNSON—175

Having a conversation with someone is complicated, if you don't know who you're talking to.

Our Prayer Team is *divine*. Our Father loves us; our Savior, Jesus, intercedes and advocates for us; and our Holy Spirit groans, comforts, leads, and teaches us.

How to Use This Book

Over the years, I've read books on prayer that left me feeling burdened, with less of a desire to pray. I thought, *I'm doing something wrong. I'm not intense enough, sincere enough. I wish I could be more like the author.* My desire is that after you read these journeys, your prayer times will become more peaceful. Because we have a divine Prayer Team, I pray you will feel lighter, and you will enter His throne room and rest—rather than wrestle—and be blessed.

At your own pace, you can explore the variety of sisters' prayer journeys here alongside the Scriptures. Consider the prayer prompts and opportunities to reflect on your own time-frame, whether you use this as a prayer devotional, personal or small-group study, or journaling help.

These journeys are our unadulterated testimonies. Since God's love has changed our lives, we don't mind revealing these transforming prayer journeys. Like the home-renovations I enjoy watching—the property owners don't mind presenting the wrecked room, building, or yard beforehand because they know the results *after* the transformation are amazing—our stories are revealing, too, and we hope helpful.

In the process of developing *Blessed Is She*, God gave me this image: a wall of women praying, weeping, and calling out; daughters, sisters, mothers, grandmothers, and aunties pleading on behalf of themselves and their loved ones, friends, and strangers. These journeys are testimonies that confirm God not only hears our pleas but He is our sure foundation. His generous love blesses each and every one of us all the time. As we comprehend this love, we grasp intimate conversation with the One who knows just how to respond, even before we finish calling on Him!

These days, I'm just asking God to quiet my heart. I just want to linger longer in His presence. Listening . . . not waiting so much for marching orders for the day. I'm finding pleasure in prayer. Feeling all right when I prayerfully nap in God's throne room. God told us, "Be still, and *know* that I am God" (Psalm 46:10, emphasis mine). We don't need to stand at attention like soldiers!

We can simply be like a sleepy-headed child, silently resting our spirit in the palm of our Father's hand. He reminds us to lay down our anxieties and stop scrambling to get busy building up our part in His kingdom work. We can sit still, amazed at who God is and what He is already doing, rather than constantly asking, *what do you want* me *to do?* As we draw close, believing in His love for us, we know He is with us. As we pray, He is already praying for us.

About Our Journeys

My pillow hit the floor for the second time. Granny's squinting eyes peered in my direction. She knew I was watching, but neither of us said a word. Unlike the middle of the day when Granny constantly found a job for me to do. "Sally" (my nickname), "Go get my glasses off my night table." Or, "Sally, go to the grocery store next door and get me four slices of baloney and a loaf of bread." Tonight, no requests or conversations. Granny and I knew this was God's time.

My half-asleep head hung over the edge of the twin rollaway at the end of Granny's bed. As I lay there observing her, I fought hard against the "Sandman" (our name for sleepiness). My grandmother on her knees in prayer fascinated me. Granny, me, and my older sister Debra had already talked to God together. We had asked the Lord to meet the needs of our parents, aunts, uncles, cousins, church members, everybody in-between, including "the spooky man," who walked around the neighborhood. After we concluded our prayers and Granny said, "Goodnight," she remained on her knees.

While I drifted and drowsed, I noticed Grandma's head bobbing and her lips moving rapidly. I strained to hear a word, but the room remained silent. I *felt* her inaudible words. I wondered, *what are they going on about—her and God? What more does she have to say to Him? What are their secrets?* I wanted to be in those conversations, to know what she and God discussed long into the night.

I don't remember ever asking her any questions about those late-night sessions. My grandmother died shortly after

I celebrated my tenth birthday. Now, decades later, I have a greater understanding of those nights. God allowed Granny to be a part of the spiritual pathway He had planned for me. The Holy Spirit had stirred my heart, speaking gently to me while I observed my grandmother, her life informing my journey.

ELIZABETH PAVED THE WAY FOR MARY

I'm sure I've read the story a hundred times, of the angel visiting Mary and her going to see her cousin Elizabeth. Combing over this familiar Bible passage, I observe afresh how God arranged for Elizabeth, possibly in her sixties, seventies, or even eighties, to experience a miraculous-though-natural conception six months before her cousin Mary's supernatural conception (Luke 1:12–20). Elizabeth had several months to mull over God's phenomenal plan, empowering this older woman to encourage this young girl's understanding of God's intervention. When Mary appeared at her door, Elizabeth and *the baby within her* responded. John the Baptist, Jesus's forerunner, leaped inside Elizabeth's womb. Then Elizabeth called Mary, the mother of the Messiah, "blessed" (Luke 1:42). The older woman commended the younger for surrendering her yes to the Lord for whatever He had in mind (Luke 1:45).

Diane Reeder introduces us to that scene:

> *The angel had already assured Mary, "You have nothing to fear" (Luke 1:30). "God has a surprise for you:*

> *You will become pregnant and give birth to a son and*
> *call his name Jesus."* . . . *"But how?" replied Mary.*
> *"I've never slept with a man.* . . . *Yes, I see it all now:*
> *I'm the Lord's maid, ready to serve. Let it be with me*
> *just as you say."* (see LUKE 1:26–37 MSG)

Mary knew her Creator. She was humble and obedient to God, and we should follow her example. Yet, there is more to Mary than this middle part of the book of Luke, where she bows in obedience to such a strange request borne by the angel of the Lord, who represents God himself. Indeed, she was afraid and humble. But what happened when she visited her cousin, Elizabeth? The angel reinforced and rewarded Mary's faith by bearing another good news tiding: her cousin would be the vessel for yet another God-miracle as Elizabeth was carrying—past the age of child-bearing—Jesus's cousin! Mary was visibly thrilled and put on her traveling shoes to her cousin's house. When she said, "Hey, Elizabeth!" or whatever greeting was customary in that day, the future prophet John leaped in Elizabeth's womb.

After all, God had already ordained John, not yet fully formed, a prophet. Nevertheless, John had the Spirit in him, and that Spirit sensed the presence of Jesus, even less developed, in Mary's womb. These two women-vessels, significant bearers of God's good news, were *blessed* to witness in each other the filling of the Holy Spirit. These praying women listened to God, and God himself prophesied through them.

Mary heard from God, and she talked back to Him with her questions and even her fears. That is the essence of sincere prayer. Such an unbelievably brilliant gift—Jesus Christ—given through a woman who listened to and responded to God, and dared to take Him at His word.

When Mary entered Elizabeth and Zacharias's home, I believe the couple began educating Mary about what God was showing her, as well as helping her to understand the Messianic Scriptures, such as in Isaiah 7:14. Mary and Elizabeth both stepped into what the Lord had already arranged.

OTHERS PAVED THE WAY FOR US

The power of the Holy Spirit guided my grandmother's conversations each night as she leaned into the warm blanket of God's love wrapped around her. She drew on this strength for her footsteps each new day. She needed His help to accomplish all of her daily activities, including caring for her daughter, who was paralyzed from her waist down and in a wheelchair. And Granny was babysitter to her grandchildren and cared for children in the neighborhood. On top of all of that, she ran a laundry business out of her home.

There was no way I was ready for a talk about prayer after a day of *my* adventures. At four or five years old, I spent my days riding in a Red Flyer wagon, falling off bikes, catching fireflies, and playing outside until I heard my name called for supper. But as I watched Granny at night, God had me in His classroom. He fulfilled what He intended. In my early years, how much could my grandmother have tutored me about her journey with the

Lord? How much could she have verbally explained about her nightly prayers? However, she proved to be a role model; one of the instruments in the Lord's hand to draw me to himself. Like Mary and Elizabeth, I merely stepped into what God had planned and provided. God always has and always will provide, including in prayer.

I recited an old Puritan prayer from 1711, something quick, rhythmic, and easy for a child: "Now I lay me down to sleep, I pray the Lord my soul to keep. If I should die before I wake, I pray the Lord my soul to take." As an adult, I heard people debating whether one should say such a prayer to a child, speaking of dying in the night. I said this prayer without fear. I found it comforting to know that if the "boogeyman" tried to get me at night, God was prepared to rescue and take me safely to heaven.

Later, I learned the Lord's Prayer and Psalm 23, since the Lord's Prayer was sung at every service and wedding I attended, while Psalm 23 was quoted at funerals. They were not difficult to memorize. Their words became a natural fabric of my life. Growing up, I heard and recited both in church, and early in my teen years, I learned the difference between being a church *attender* and becoming a *member* of God's family. I became a Christian. I trusted Christ for my salvation rather than my name merely written on a church roll. I understood Jesus died on Calvary for me and my sin. My entrance into heaven and being able to stand before the Father were because of Jesus's work on the cross, and not my own merit or self-effort. For the first time, I comprehended Paul's words to the church in Ephesus: "For by grace are ye saved through faith;

and that not of yourselves: it is the gift of God: Not of works, lest any man should boast" (Ephesians 2:8–9).

The day I prayed and talked all this over with the Lord, I acknowledged Jesus's heart of love and His sacrifice, as He opened my heart to himself. My view of God, church, the Bible, fellow Christians, and even unbelievers changed. I wanted everyone to take a dip in God's love and understand how He demonstrates it through Christ's death on the cross. I experienced the Lord's compassion as I read Scripture. The incidents in the Bible were no longer stories about ancient characters but flowed into a better understanding of God and His plan and desire to work through people, by making them new in Christ (see 2 Corinthians 5:17).

HAPPY DAY

My prayer life took a drastic turn after coming into relationship with God through Christ. I no longer gave God a laundry list of what I needed Him to do for me; I prayed more for others. Mrs. Smith, my pastor's wife, helped me understand more about the gospel as she taught me how to *study* the Bible. I learned how to converse with God—listening to Him as I expressed my heart.

My pastor conducted a prayer workshop. I learned the importance of praying *for others*, especially for people to understand what it means to have a relationship with Jesus Christ. I filled my workshop manual with the name of every unsaved friend and relative I could think of, from California to New York, longing for them to also enter into relationship with Christ. I was excited!

Years later, I found that manual in the basement and felt ashamed because I had stopped praying for many of those listed in the book. As far as I knew, many of them remained unbelievers. I felt the weight of my forgetfulness, even thinking of it as prayer negligence. But one summer, I was preparing to speak before a group of leaders about Bible study and evangelism when God whispered to my heart in the middle of my prayer.

I stood before an audience of mature Christians who were well-versed in the Scriptures. Nervous and having sweated bullets for months before my scheduled speech — everybody and their mama had been praying for me. But minutes before I advanced to the podium, this horrible thought went through my mind: *What if the intercessors I asked to pray for me all forgot?* I would have sent a group-text to remind everyone, but I had no access. In place of my panic, Jesus spoke to my heart, *If they all forget, I did not forget. I am in heaven praying for you.* Wow.

I began to comprehend then what I now know deeply:

- God loves me, prays for me, and longs to commune with me because of the richness of His mercy (Ephesians 2:4). This has transformed my heart on this Christian journey, to understand that growth and development are not completely my responsibility.
- Jesus is my Mediator communicating what is on the Father's heart to me, and my heart to Him (Romans 8:34).

- The Holy Spirit is praying for me; the Scripture says, with groaning so deep, no one can understand (Romans 8:26).

As I progress in prayer, I am less talkative in my prayer time. I spend more time asking Jesus what He and the Father are discussing. *What do you want to communicate to me, or do you want me to sit here, be quiet, and rest awhile?*

I used to be anxious, thinking, *I got it, I know what you want, and I'm on it.* You know, this attitude some of us cannot get free of. I believe, for African American women, it has been going on since slavery. When slave masters sold away our men, we felt the burden, and we had to take charge. We were responsible for everybody from the field hands to the master in the big house. Cheryl L. Woods-Giscombé calls this the "Superwoman Schema" in her research on "African American Women's Views on Stress, Strength, and Health." Ours is a complex history; however, it's fair to say that legalized slavery forced women to take on roles necessary for survival. Compromised and disenfranchised Black men were left with limited ability to provide financial and emotional support to their partners and families.

Still, all too often, mothers carry the burden of working, caring for children, and managing the home. This attitude can transfer into our spiritual life: going, doing, moving, fixing. We may tell the Lord, *I got this. I'm working it out at home, on my job, at church, in the community. If I'm not holding up everybody and everything, the whole shebang just might collapse.* But some of us are dying inside. So, here lately, I find myself taking the "Be still" Scriptures to heart.

"Be still, and know that I am God!" (Psalm 46:10 NLT). God gave this command after the children of Israel left Egypt. The Red Sea in front of them and the angry Egyptian army hot on their tails. Talk about a rock and a hard place. I'm sure everything in them wanted to run, holler, scream, go crazy—and the Father told His children, "Hush, don't move, and watch me work this out" (Exodus 14:14, paraphrase).

God continually reminds us to lay down our anxieties. I've gotten tired of scrambling. I want to sit; amazed at God's activity, praising what God is already doing. How about you?

—VICTORIA

Blessed
WITH A DIVINE PRAYER TEAM

IN HIS PRESENCE

I call my father early every morning. During our time, Dad and I talk about many things, laugh, and share our love for one another. At times I serenade my dad. Other moments, I offer comfort and spark a memory from when I was a young girl.

One day I was rushing to work . . . and forgot to call. Later that morning, Dad called and asked, "Cynthia, did you forget about me?"

"Oh, no, my mind was on what I had to do at work today and I forgot."

"I know you have things to do and you are busy, but I was waiting for you to call me. I wanted to talk to you," he said.

I apologized and promised to keep our calls because these talks fill my heart with joy and mean so much to him. His was a gentle reminder of how our heavenly Father feels about us.

In the garden of Eden, God looked for Adam and Eve: "Where are you?" (Genesis 3:9 NLT). God wanted to talk with His people. He has always desired for us to be with Him. He has established our fellowship for that reason. He understands our lives, and He is seeking, calling, and waiting for us.

— CYNTHIA ATKINS

Providing True Love

Imagine for a few minutes all your secret thoughts and actions no one knows anything about. You know, the private things you've said in your head. Now project those thoughts and actions on a movie screen. God has seen our movies, and He still loves and wants to provide for us, even on our worst days.

On one of the worst days of my life, I broke this sad news to my young children: "Your father and I have separated. Your dad will not be living here anymore." After the door closed and they left for school, I pictured God's face: angry, disappointed. I envisioned Him walking through the house (like my biological father used to do), criticizing, "You always messing something up and then I have to come along and fix it." My dad took care of me as a good, responsible parent, and had attended most of the significant events in my life. But I also remember him being angry, disappointed, and often critical of me. Initially, this is how I envisioned my heavenly Father—a provider always wishing I'd do better.

Years later God took me back to that day and gently said, *That was not me; Victoria, I love you. I sat on the step next to you, weeping, holding your broken heart in my hand.* Now looking back, I ask myself, *how in the world did I get that ugly face on God when He is so unlike that?*

When I reflect on my early years of struggling to pray, it's hard to believe the false face I placed on God. Comprehending *who* we're talking to is crucial to prayer. We need to *see* God's loving heart. Imagine being at the top of His prayer list. He tenderly writes our names in His prayer book. Yes, your name is etched on each page in big bold letters at the top, around the sides, and at the bottom, He's said He's crazy about you (see Isaiah 49:16).

I asked a Bible teacher once, "If God loves us so much, why doesn't He write that out plainly on every page in Scripture?" She responded, "He did." I had a puzzled look. I had studied my Bible for intellectual knowledge, attempting to comprehend people, events, and concepts. Eventually, God began showing me the love behind all those words and stories.

Let's note God's reaction to Eve after her sin in the garden. I don't think there's anyone who would disagree, sister girl messed up. God placed her and Adam in a beautiful, perfect environment. I picture them running freely among the animals, swimming in the ocean without the threat of drowning, lying in a field of fragrant flowers, and looking up at the heavens.

That all ended. The enemy tricked them, twisted God's words, and enticed them to eat from the forbidden tree (Genesis 3:1–6). After their blaming, God, in His abundant love and grace, provided a necessary sacrifice for His first couple (Genesis 3:21). He declared the coming Savior would one day crush Satan (Genesis 3:15). And after God expelled Adam and Eve from the garden, we see the Father helped Eve as she delivered her first child (Genesis 4:1). We see His judgment but also His love and forgiveness for their transgression. He loved them. He still loves, in such a grand way.

My three-year-old grandson teaches me about our Father's grand love. Ian usually comes into my house full of life. He races around, plays with cars, picks his guitar, sings, attempts to write his name while talking away, running back and forth from me to Grandpa, and asking for cookies, chips, and juice. But then there are days when he comes in sad. "Where is Daddy? Is Mama coming?" He does not want to take off his shoes and get comfortable. I offer him a cracker, a peanut-butter sandwich, a glass of milk, and the answer is, "No, no, no." About seven o'clock in the evening, I'll ask this toddler, "Is it time for bubbles?" He heads upstairs; he loves to get in the tub and play with his bath toys. We dress him in his favorite plaid pajamas and he settles into my lap. We sing Jesus songs until he falls asleep. I linger over his curly hair and pray.

It does not matter whether Ian comes in happy-go-lucky, or sad, weepy, and whining; I'm going to provide. Granny is still going to feed him and see that he gets what he needs.

God is so much more steadfast. Faithful and unmoved by our fickleness. His attributes do not fluctuate. One day I am praising and thanking God all day. But the next day I am tired, depressed, and discouraged, expressing my anger. *Lord, why have I been in the waiting room so long?*

The Father refuses to withhold His love; He's not upset because we have our hand on our hip, voicing our frustration about His "lack of quickness." God compassionately yearns for closeness with us. That's embedded in who He is. The Father still loves me, always looking out for me because I am His child. The welcome sign in the throne room is never taken down, even when my prayer room door displays its sign, "Out to Lunch."

When God's love is mentioned in the Bible, it's often coupled with words like *steadfast, mercy, faithful,* or *endureth* (see

Psalm 118:1–4). God's steadfast love is a constant affection, an enduring kindness, graciousness, mercy; His compassion never fails (Lamentations 3:22–23). It's complicated to define because no other love compares; nothing comes close to God's love for us. It is deep, sealed with His covenant and over-whelming compassion. You can depend on it one hundred percent. It is always there as promised, without fail. Our daily lives change; how great it is to know God, who is unchanged by our crazy world.

Mind you, God is not under obligation to love in this way. He chooses to love us—the same way Jesus decided to go to the cross, to die for the sin of mankind and demonstrate the Fathers' love. This is the love He lavishes on us each and every day.

The day I realized the loving heart of God demonstrated through Jesus on the cross, I invited Him into my heart. At that moment my caretaker changed; I gained a heavenly Father who provides for me rather than me attempting to do so.

When Jesus's disciples asked Him to teach them to pray, He started out with the unusual Jewish title for God, "Our Father." The reference Jesus used recognized the Lord as holy, mighty, sovereign, God of the universe. "Our Father" resides in another realm, ruling over all, but at the same time, near to His children, caring for us. The disciples marveled at this special bond Jesus demonstrated as He prayed. I do too.

Jewish men were exposed to many ritualistic devotions throughout their lives. Did they need another "how to pray" lesson? They did not think so until they observed Jesus's prayer life. It made them hungry for what Jesus graciously allowed them to enter into. He wanted them to hear, and we share the same Father.

Today, has prayer been reduced to a laundry list placed before God's face? I don't know about you, but I sometimes have had to reconsider my conversations with God. I had a conversation with God while writing this:

SINGING OVER US

"Lord?"

Yes, Victoria.

"Uh, I have a problem."

Yes?

"Uh, well maybe it's not a problem; more like a question."

Yes, ask away.

"Well, you know I am writing this book on prayer, and in the months that I have been working on it a lot of the families I have been praying for . . . their situations are getting worse, not better."

Right.

"You already know. Brother-in-law had major heart surgery. My mother got pneumonia—again. Another friend had routine hip surgery, but it turned out more severe than expected. One friend is texting me now from a hotel after a severe domestic-violence incident in her home. One friend's son was found dead on the street in the middle of winter a few weeks ago. One friend was hopeful about a relationship, only to be heartbroken. And did I mention the serious health issue

I'm dealing with? Got everybody praying for me but nothing is changing."

So you want to fill your prayer book with stories about how you prayed for people and for yourself, and then all these wonderful things happened because of your prayers.

"Well, yeah. It does not have to be the whole book, but I at least wanted to report some good news because of prayer."

OK, let me get this straight; you want to communicate in your prayer book, "you pray, and the Santa Claus God in the sky answers and gives you what you want." Like getting gifts on Christmas, big and expensive.

"Ouch. Do you have to say it like that? Makes me seem like I only pray to get what I want."

Mmm.

"OK, Father. I am back in Prayer 101. Here is your marker for the board. I am taking my seat with the computer open, ready to take notes."

All right. Let's erase the board and start fresh. Click on Zephaniah 3:17.

"Oh, Lord, you have given that to me so many times, I do not even need to look it up. 'The LORD thy God in the midst of thee is mighty; he will save, he will rejoice over thee with joy; he will rest in his love, he will joy over thee with singing.'

"I know, you are with me, a mighty God. You've saved me; you are thrilled with me, you love me, and you are singing over me, right now."

Mmm, you have learned well. Now for your homework assignment.

"What, homework?"

Yes. All day today I want you to listen to that verse with your head and your heart, then listen for my song.

"Mmm."

Now that, my child, is prayer.

Anyone else need to ask God's forgiveness for turning prayer time into a laundry list of "I wants"? Sometimes I am so involved with arranging the prayer requests on the throne room table, I have not even looked up to acknowledge who is sitting at the head. I fail to investigate His heart, and observe His love, grace, and mercy. Reckless, I run right over His words, desires, and feelings. Thank God for His patience as He teaches us about prayer. Let's unpack more of Zephaniah 3:17.

"The LORD thy God in the midst of thee." Throughout the Old Testament, God demonstrated His desire to dwell among His humans. In the garden, He walked and talked with Adam and Eve (Genesis 3:8). He instructed Moses to build a tabernacle, and for David's son Solomon to build a temple (Exodus 25:8; 1 Kings 6:1). Both the temple and the tabernacle symbolized God's desire to commune with His people.

In this life, there is a lot to be afraid of, and Christians can grow faint and weary. But there's good news! God chooses to be with us every step of the way. Our God is almighty, ruler of all, and possesses infinite power.

"He will save." God put flesh on himself and came in the form of Jesus Christ to die on the cross to save the lost. Jesus's

death saves us from sin, Satan, and hell. And He gave the Holy Spirit to dwell with us and see to it that we make it all the way home, to be with Him forever.

"He will rejoice over thee." I think that one of the best parts of any wedding is watching the groom watch his bride come down the aisle, decked out in her wedding attire. There is joy on God's face when He looks at His children and is full of admiration and compassion that never changes.

"Calm all your fears" (NLT). The thought of resting in God's love and allowing Him to calm us down is a beautiful thought and expression. The reality is that the Father is not trying His best or working hard at loving us; instead, it is His pleasure.

"He rejoices over thee with singing." When I told another Christian sister about this verse, she began to laugh. She immediately started flipping the pages of her Bible to read the verse for herself. "I never heard anything like that," she said, "God singing over us." I had felt the same way when I first heard this verse. I picture with immense pleasure God rocking me, singing me a lullaby, soothing me.

I used to think I had to sing to *Him* and learn how to worship. It was a new day when I discovered God sings over me; I simply need to join in. *Hallelujah.* Sometimes when I'm having a horrible, very bad day, I stop and say, "Lord, what are you singing over me right now?" He always brings a song to mind, and I begin to sing. This has turned into such a sweet thing between us.

In life, for so many years of my Christian walk, I had concentrated on God being a disciplinarian. I skipped over a lot of the "I love you" verses in the Bible, thinking I constantly displeased Him. It took a while for me to understand the Lord's delight over me as His child. He holds me in the palm of His loving hand. He's not wagging an accusing finger in my face or yours. Though, people may accuse:

"SHE'S THE ONE . . ."

She's the one that got pregnant before she got married.
She's the one with two baby daddies.
She's the one that got the abortion.
She's the one who can't get off drugs.
She's the one that was in the homeless shelter.
She's the one who had to call the church to pay her gas bill.
She's the one who got fired.
She's the one who can't keep a job.
She's the one who had an affair.
She's the one putting up with her womanizing husband.
She's the one who got evicted from her apartment.
She's the one who was showing too much on the internet.
She's the one who was in foster care.
She's the one who was adopted.
She's the one who got molested.
She's the one who got raped.
She's the one who went to prison.
She's the one whose boyfriend gave her a black eye.
She's the one who's had several divorces and remarriages.
She's the one who's been in a mental hospital.
She's the one whose child sells drugs.

She's the one who abused her child.

She's the one who let her boyfriend abuse her child.

She's the one living with that man, but they are not married.

She's the one who went to jail.

She's the one _____ .

Go ahead. If your situation is missing, feel free to use the blank space to add to the list. Find yourself on the list. I'm on there—several times. Take a moment to experience the finger-pointing, and to relive any shame. Hear the *I told you so?* You know, *I told you not to go there . . . I told you not to get hooked up with him . . . You never listen . . . You so hardheaded . . .*

Who are your accusers? Your mama, daddy, church folks, or neighbors? Maybe even your best friend, the love of your life, your husband, or a special someone else? I'll tell you one place shaming accusations do not come from—our loving heavenly Father! He convicts but He does not condemn us, because of Christ (Romans 7:25–8:1).

—VICTORIA

Reflect

God initiates a prayerful conversation with the kind of delighting spirit reflected in Zephaniah 3:17. What is your response?

Why do you think it's essential to know God's love is the first leg of our prayer experience? What difference does that make?

33

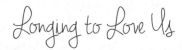
Longing to Love Us

"God, save me!" I cried as I fell to my knees in the middle of my dusty garage. Seventeen, I knelt on the ground, crying and pleading, not realizing I was experiencing the work of the Holy Spirit. I had hit rock bottom, literally, in the consequences of my bad choices. Looking back, I can see that.

Growing up, I was aware of God, though I didn't see Him in my life. Some of my earliest memories include seeing my mother baptized and attending my babysitter's church. Labeling my family *religious* or *Christian* would be a stretch. My mother taught me about God in practical ways and had a profound impact as I witnessed her praying at her bedside every morning. However, other than praying at breakfast and reciting the prayer, "Now, I lay me down to sleep," I did not understand the power of prayer or have a personal relationship with God.

In addition to my mother, my grandmother and aunt were vital in my upbringing. However, my father was not around. I had many interactions with my dad during my early childhood, but the damage of infidelity and sin plagued my parents' relationship. They found themselves in a vicious cycle of break-up and make-up. Eventually, my dad married again. Sadly, I got caught in the middle. My relationship with him became a casualty of their warfare. He and his new wife began to build their family, while I became a shadow of his past. Instead of time with him, I received broken and empty promises. Every so often I would be invited to his house, but that stopped when I was about eight years old. Suddenly, my father told me, "My wife is uncomfortable with you," and I was no longer welcome in their home.

Despite the broken relationship with my dad, I continued to function in what I would call a healthy way. I excelled academically and in extracurricular activities. I had friendships with everyone, but I was unable to commit to any one group. When I turned sixteen, my behavior reflected the effects of growing up without a father. The lyrics to my favorite song, "No Daddy" by Teairra Mari: "I ain't had no daddy around when I was growing up; that's why I'm wild, and I don't give . . . " This song was relevant, and became my anthem and excuse for my behavior.

I became angry, wild, and rebellious as a broken teenager searching for love in all the wrong places. I searched for love in unhealthy relationships, sports, and eventually harmful substances to temporarily fill the painful void in my heart. Not knowing that I could not find what I looked for in these ways. I experienced mood swings, going from a state of emotional satisfaction to volatile anger and self-loathing. I struggled with the fact that I looked *just like my father* and that my mother called me a "daddy's girl." *A daddy's girl,* I thought to myself. *He does not want anything to do with me.*

By the age of seventeen, my behavior spiraled into an on-again-off-again-on-again relationship with a typical bad boy; he had been to jail, hung out on the streets selling drugs, and drank. He provided me with attention I thought was the love I had been missing. I followed him, regardless of what he did. It started with drinking—and escalated to me being an accomplice to several of his crimes. No one saw it coming.

I had three criminal cases pending against me, and two were felonies. I had never been in this type of trouble in my life, and felt utterly alone. I rebelled against my mother and moved out to be with my boyfriend. He bounced back and forth between the mother of his unborn child and me. The only person I felt I could depend on was myself. I remember my nonchalant attitude about the situation: *I do not really care about what happens to me. I am glad my future is not up to me at the moment.*

I remember sitting in a detective's office after participating in a crime; guilty as charged. I will never forget the female detective looking me in the face, telling how she had been in my exact situation: fallen for a no-good guy, doing anything to cover for him. She pleaded, "Let this go, let him go." But I remained stubborn. I lied to her, just as he told me to. I watched disappointment wash over her face. As I walked out, I remember thinking, *I will be arrested in a matter of days.* Instead, days turned into weeks and weeks into months, with no sign of legal trouble or jail time. But I had to always "look over my shoulder."

Covered in shame, I moved back home with my mom. Regretting so many past decisions, I sat on the couch thinking *my life is over.* I then attempted to commit suicide. Methodically gathering every pill in the house and taking them, I sat there sobbing. And then I realized I did not want my mom to come into the house and find me dead. So, I called the police to report a suicide. I did not know the 911 operator would send paramedics. Within minutes they burst into my front door, administered life-saving drugs, and transported me to the hospital.

When I awoke at the hospital, I saw my mother—and my father. He cried, "This is all my fault." My heart waxed cold towards him at that moment. I thought, *how dare you think you are that important that I would make life or death decisions because of you.* I sat silent, waiting to pass a psych exam and go home. Inexplicably, they decided against the mental health test and let me leave within a few hours.

As we left the hospital, my mom received an outpouring of messages on her cell phone. Her grandmother unexpectedly died in the very moments when doctors were attempting to save my life. My thoughts reflected on our last time together. I had shown up on her porch for a visit while I was out on the street. She was sure that I was on drugs. Later that night she had told my mom, "I am praying for God to work in Breezy's life and bring her back." The severity of the moment and the divine timing hit me.

A year passed following that meeting in the detective's office. Finally, the law enforcement officer's words, my suicide attempt, and the death of my great-grandmother came together in the garage that day. I suddenly became overjoyed with how good God had been to me. I realized that, through all my mess, He was still there and that He somehow loved me. Emotionally overwhelmed, that's why I fell to my knees and called out to God. That day the Spirit of God moved in my life, and I began to reflect on His influence throughout my childhood and up to that very moment. Though I had misunderstood His presence before, I started to see His grace in a whole new way. He had saved my life.

The beginning of my personal prayer journey was rugged. Though I stood firm concerning my salvation through Jesus, and I knew God's love for me, I approached Him in fear. I thought, *any wrong move and He will cast me out, just like I was cast out of my natural father's presence.* By my mid-twenties, I began to experience God as my Father, who wants good for me.

I sat one day reading the Lord's Prayer, and it hit me. Jesus told us, "Pray like this: Our Father . . ." (Matthew 6:9 NLT). *Our Father* stuck out, and I began repeating those two words. I felt Jesus inviting me into the fold of God's family. He spoke to my heart, "Breonna, you're no longer a slave or an indebted servant; you are a daughter of God." I became enthralled with that notion—*God's daughter? Me?* This new thought also challenged me to ask, *what is the right relationship with the heavenly Father? What does that really look like?*

FATHERHOOD

I began to study fatherhood. I noticed the love, identity, hope, and inspiration fathers provide to their children. I consumed Bible verses teaching about the Father's love for us: "So if you sinful people know how to give good gifts to your children, how much more will your heavenly Father give good gifts to those who ask him" (Matthew 7:11 NLT).

Jesus's statement about prayer illuminated my mind, "Therefore I say unto you, what things soever ye desire, when ye pray, believe that ye receive them, and ye shall have them" (Mark 11:24). Suddenly the light switched on. I now understood and believed God and the truth of His Word. My heavenly Father was *my* Father, and promised to provide for me.

God demonstrated such patience with me as I explored and questioned the meaning of this fatherhood relationship with Him. My confidence began to grow and strengthen. When I prayed, my words expressed my heart to heaven. God constantly showed and reminded me, *you are my child.* I understood He sincerely desires a relationship with me, so I cultivated that relationship through prayer.

MY LIFELINE

Today, prayer is my lifeline. People often come to me for prayer because of the boldness and tenacity God has given me to approach Him. Sometimes I will catch myself on my knees, and I chuckle because I remember seeing my mom in that same posture when I was a little girl. I think of my great-grandmother who was a prayer warrior, in the same posture, praying for me during my rebellion. I am committed to living a life of prayer, knowing that Jesus is living and is interceding on my behalf (Hebrews 7:25). I realize, without a doubt, I'm saved because of the prayers of other people. Now I willingly pray for others, as I am *His* child.

I like to pray in spoken word, and my experiences seem to resonate with many in the audiences. This prayer is a thank-you to God for His transformation:

CHILD OF THE KING

Abandoned then adopted

Broken then restored

Rejected then accepted

Scarred but made new

Doomed then redeemed

I am the child of the King

Chosen since before time by the Highest to do a great thing

Once torn down by the world and the deceit of the enemy

Believing I was left behind, defeated and disjointed

But my Father has chosen, anointed, and appointed me

Me. The one who watched everything
I thought was good be demolished

Me. Treated like a black leather shoe unpolished for the streets and
frowned upon everywhere else

Spent countless nights wishing I could be anybody but myself

Until I realized that I am the child of the King

Until I learned the dissemination of grace that seemed to hit
everybody but me was really my portion

That I was forgiven of my sins

He canceled out the shame of a lifetime of purpose abortion

He honestly did work it out for my good
using every piece of my story

That He would take the deepest darkest places and
illuminate them for His glory

My God. He took every burden, broke every chain, freed me of
yokes, and removed the mind monsters from my brain

Glory to the King, through His transformative power
I will never be the same

Restored to my place of dominion and authority
over creation I'll reign

All because of Jesus, my Savior, who laid down His life
so that I would have it more abundantly

The one who performed miracles as our blueprint and said
we do greater works than He

The Lord of Lords when we were blind made us see,
deaf let us hear, far drew us near, mute let us talk
On the water showed us to walk and said to use
our faith to move mountains

The one who called us to repent and spoke to our unseen

Released the Holy Spirit and called us redeemed

Made us joint-heirs to the kingdom. Our Father is the king; the ruler
of the new heaven and the new earth

Washed away my transgressions and gave me a new birth

That is why I am no longer abandoned, rejected,
broken, scarred or doomed

I am adopted, accepted, restored, and made new and redeemed.

— BREONNA ROSTIC

Empowering Us

I had always found it hard to pray because I never felt like God wanted me in His presence. I mistakenly thought I was disqualified, brought nothing, or brought too much baggage. Though I was born and raised in a Christian family, much of the prayer I had seen happened at church, in *front* of the congregation. And the church members who prayed seemed to have a title in front of their names. I carried no designation, and felt irrelevant and unimportant. *How could someone like me come to such a great God? Why would such an awesome God want to hear from me?* Those thoughts and feelings were barriers to an intimate prayer relationship with the Father.

When I hit a dark season of depression as a young adult, I longed to pray, to run into God's presence, pour out my heart before Him, and allow Him to minister to me, but had no idea where to begin. I thought, *how do I start or what words do I say?* I had moved alone to a new city, had little access to family or friends, and my car had been repossessed. On top of everything, I was recovering from a bad relationship. I needed God.

I sat in the middle of my empty apartment with my face flooded with tears. *How do I begin to tell God how lost I feel? About my loneliness?* And then I felt this gentle presence wooing me to pour out everything before God. His love was so profound for me at that moment. I needed Him, and He was already there. I had an Ephesians 3 encounter with the Father:

> *Then Christ will make his home in your hearts as*
> *you trust in him. Your roots will grow down into*

God's love and keep you strong. And may you have the power to understand, as all God's people should, how wide, how long, how high, and how deep his love is. May you experience the love of Christ, though it is too great to understand fully. Then you will be made complete with all the fullness of life and power that comes from God. (EPHESIANS 3:17–19 NLT)

That was the beginning of my becoming rooted and grounded in His love. Prayer became a safe place for me during this season of my life—it wasn't just something I *did*; it was something I learned to *live*. I didn't need a title to pray, any particular words, or an audience; just the Father and me. The closeness I now enjoy with God in prayer developed out of experiencing His love. He opened the corridors of my heart and showed me where there was more room to receive His love. I felt the breadth, length, depth, and height of His passion and it consumed my entire being. My soul knows God longs for me to dwell in His presence. He is with me, listening and loving. When I quiet myself, I can hear Him speaking to my heart.

I believe He longs to spend time with me in prayer and awaits my arrival. He beckons me to come to Him, whether I arrive crying, angry, confused, or frustrated. The Father assures me that I won't leave His presence the way I entered. I always leave better. This doesn't mean I get my way, or that He works some instantaneous miracle. However, it is that moment in His presence where I am reminded of how great His love is for me. His love empowers me to live another day, literally.

— JOLANDA ROGERS

Reflect

Recall a time or a season in your life when you doubted God's love for you.

What was your turning point?

Take a moment and thank God for lovingly guiding and rescuing you from situations.

Or do you need to ask the Holy Spirit's help to realize what may be keeping you from experiencing God's love?

Jesus Is Praying

Morning noises from the kitchen on the first floor mingled with the smell of sizzling bacon, wafting to my upstairs bedroom: dishes clinking together and songs from Mom's radio mixed with Mom's soft humming as she fried breakfast. Awaking, I remembered the vivid nightmare that had sliced through my sleep some hours before: people running from fiery torches— and me viewing that scene from inside an earthen grave lined with mourners. (I still can't tell you how or why I had the dream because we were not churchgoers and I had not heard any preaching.) I cried, "Mom!" And she appeared at the bottom step of the stairwell looking up lovingly to me at the top. I called out, "Mom, when I die, will I be in a grave forever?" She could see my frightened young face.

"Oh, no, baby, your soul will live forever with God in heaven." Her smile reassured me. I even dozed back to sleep for a bit, remembering her prayers with me before bedtime, believing her answer to my fear, and considering God as my night watcher and soul keeper.

Mom always prayed with me, though I didn't know God or understand how to hear Him. I leaned on her petition to "lay me down to sleep." I did not know about *faith*. And my powerful father's stories caused me to question faith as foolishness. He had seen some of the same people praying in churches preach lies, slavery, and lynching. He told about relatives preaching but not practicing godliness. The only exception: his father, a slave, who served others through the Black Church.

But my mother's watchful gaze kept me on bended knees each night at bedtime. I would peek at her praying, believing in mimicking her. That's what I trusted. She continued to call on God despite my dad's righteous anger. She encouraged me to repeat "the Lord my soul to keep," freeing me to a vulnerable trust in God. I would close my prayer with *amen* and climb under the quilt in hopes that all would be well until the morning. Watching my mother's bun and apron strings disappear outside my bedroom door, I trusted her prayers. But not Jesus. Not yet.

As a child lying underneath a cozy quilt, I had no idea of the twists and turns my life would take. Life unfolds on a journey out of our control. At times, we can become like frightened children trying to find God. But God makes himself known and protects us (see Psalm 91:4; John 17:20).

FALLING INTO HIS PRESENCE

I know now that God has always, in His omniscience and love, been praying for me. And Mom agreed with Him in quiet confidence, her prayers accomplishing so much. "Confess your sins to each other and pray for each other so that you may be healed. The earnest prayer of a righteous person has great power and produces wonderful results" (James 5:16 NLT).

Mom had a lifelong relationship with Jesus. He was her Deliverer—from childhood hunger and poverty, racism, and so many other harms, including multiple assaults. She prayed sincerely, but sometimes my dad's rebuke (though I admired and loved him to death) destroyed her prayer of grace. At dinner, I remember him slamming the white table with his great, hardworking hand, making the silverware jump on Mom's secondhand-store, found-for-her-family, carefully hand-ironed-and-starched linen. Dad declared, "I put the d——— food on this table!"

He was my towering hero who had escaped the South, migrating by every means necessary. Working tirelessly seven days a week. But Mom was my beautiful heroine. She loved me on her lap, daily read me rhymes, painted green-food-color faces on my sandwich for a backyard picnic with sweet cherry Kool-Aid, mended my scuffed knees from roller-skating, curled my bangs, walked with me to the library to read a stack of books, and sent me to church with a dime wrapped in a white handkerchief.

So, I grew up divided. My parents had such different attitudes about God, and I grew up with conflicting thoughts about prayer. I definitely had no understanding of Jesus praying for me.

One Easter Sunday (one of the few days we might be in church), my mother took me to a local church. They gifted me and each of the children present with a chain engraved with the Ten Commandments. At home later, I sprawled across my bed, dangling the medallions, reading each of God's commands. And I felt doomed. Captive of guilt for breaking several of the Ten in my eight years, including when I yelled into my pillow a silent, *I hate you!* after my parents had disciplined me (they were right to correct me). I looked at the chain and began to pray more so out of fear, pleading for mercy as I sensed my sin.

My dad's rants about the church drowned my mother's prayers and efforts. He rather praised my scholastic achievement; that had been largely denied him. He had to pick cotton and plow and simply labor. He was an angry, gifted man, who wanted justice and provision for his family. So he raised me to be savvy in the world's eyes. But I was ignorant about God, impoverished in terms of intimacy while trying to understand truth. The "gospel truth" I adhered to was achievement. But I eventually learned worldly accomplishments only allow us to overcome so far. Personal success without Jesus is a "house" staked in sinking sand.

Years after graduating college, having attained influence and status, and, yes, benefiting from some opportunities, I still found myself on a lonesome road. The house of my life suffered a great fall because it had not been built on the sure foundation of faith. No godly practices; instead, I had focused on satisfying my five senses. No prayer meetings, Bible reading, or study in my youth or as an independent young adult. Instead, I earned honors, a career, a well-to-do husband, and a luxurious and lustful lifestyle.

But Jesus had already been praying for me. God's Holy Spirit spoke to my heart a clear message that lit up my insides with longing: *Is this all there is to life?* I asked myself. The Spirit prompted me: *Open that Bible and read.* And then God showed me my need as my eyes rested on the one Bible in the house that was simply a fixture in the living room in honor of an aging great aunt. I responded, opening the old, coffee-table-size Bible that wise elder had made sure was in my house. "Wine is a mocker; strong drink is raging and whosoever is deceived thereby is not wise" (Proverbs 20:1) were the first Bible words I read. *This is written directly to me and my house,* I thought. Jesus might as well have been sitting in front of me on my couch because this response was so clear: *Right, that's your lifestyle, and you're headed for trouble. You need to change. Read on.* I did and I remained in awe, even amid the changes to come.

Here is a short version of what happened next: marital separation, divorce, great loss, chronic illness, and my father's cancer, and near homelessness. But Jesus had been praying for me. And that childhood prayer about the Lord watching over my soul rescued me as an adult caring for a daughter of my own. So I began to listen to, agree with, and trust Him to keep my soul and life—no matter what. I started not only reading but believing His Word.

EVERYTHING TO GOD IN PRAYER

I became a believer in Christ at thirty, when I heard Him speak to me and read His Word, and began growing in a relationship with plenty of the same. "I was once blind" with right-now needs only Jesus could fulfill. Unforeseen, unprayed-for needs that the Lord knew about, prayed for, and settled for me, without any words from me. He knew me and my heart and all of my needs. God has continued to emphasize the truth: I can acquire material wealth and enjoy the accolades of people, but that is not enough to live on. He comes first and fulfills my every need.

Thank God for His truth.

He knows the plans He has for us, the way we will take, and how He will direct our path, our "expected end," and will guide us even when we don't understand (see Proverbs 3:5–6 and Jeremiah 29:11). God delivers us from evil and even our own motivations, turning us around, equipping us with His power, and charging us to strengthen others by sharing our faith in action (see 2 Corinthians 1:4). We can live and influence not on our own strength, but in Christ (Philippians 4:13).

The first time I fell asleep as I prayed late into the night, I awoke with a spirit of shame depressing me, until God corrected me. Now, I may fall asleep resting in prayer in the daytime, unashamed. Jesus says, *I've called you to sit with me quietly. This is your most significant work.* Simple prayer that rests in Him. He displayed this and shared with His followers to pray simple prayers while no one is watching (see Matthew 6:6).

> *"And when you pray, do not be like the hypocrites, for they love to pray standing in the synagogues and on the street corners to be seen by others. Truly I tell you, they have received their reward in full. But when you pray, go into your room, close the door and pray to your Father, who is unseen. Then your Father, who sees what is done in secret, will reward you. And when you pray, do not keep on babbling like*

pagans, for they think they will be heard because of their many words. Do not be like them, for your Father knows what you need before you ask him."
(MATTHEW 6:5–8 NIV)

THE SECRET PLACE

God knew there would come a day when I would become the caregiver to the mother who had pointed me to Christ and shown me how to pray. I remember some of the chaos but more so prayer that day. My screaming mother, in her eighties, wrestled with me on a flight of stairs. Her strong hands grabbed my shirt, and her nails scratched my chest. Confusion caused my children to run for cover. *Jesus! Jesus, what do I do now?* My mind raced. *How can I continue to live like this? How can my family, my children? I can't . . .* Then I sensed the Lord's control of the out-of-control. Jesus was with my mind and heart on those stairs amid the hurricane of emotions. There was no peace evident, but I had His peace. *Yes, call on me. You know I'm with you and will never leave you. Be patient.* And God showed himself strong in that moment and many other challenging moments throughout my mother's remaining years, even when I was weak.

Years later, when she was near death, Mom sometimes forgot who I was, and she was going blind. But when I gave her the first few words of her favorite psalm, she always responded with enthusiasm. I would say, "He that dwelleth . . ." And she would respond, "in the secret place of the most High shall abide under the shadow of the Almighty" (Psalm 91:1). And she would pray as though God was kneeling right there with her. He was.

My elderly mother continued to experience God in prayer as she suffered through Alzheimer's, declined in her body, and inclined more and more in His Spirit. On the night she passed from this life to resurrection life, at just the right time, God spoke to my heart, again. He said to my mind, *It's time*, and we immediately went to her side. As she left her earthly body and my arms, she joined God in His, and we each experienced God's presence, power, and peace.

During that season, while completing curriculum for a women's retreat that year, these and other personal experiences punctuated my perspective on issues women face and our need to look to our High Priest during trials at home, church, and in our various circumstances, including failing health and the death of loved ones. All of life points us to God's power, love, and grace. He intercedes, restores, renews, and reconfigures us. In the process of self-examination, Bible study, prayer, and contemplation through these challenges, God makes clear to us the principles of prayer He provides for our maintenance, growth, and contentment in Christ.

God can draw us from the pit of despair to himself. He can care for us on paths that lead through valleys of loss and provide His joy and restoration. God intercedes for us and provides for our relationship with Him through daily devotional time. This deepens prayer, study, and personal application of

His Word. He challenges us to greater humility and service. As we recognize our relationship with Christ, as biblical women did, we overcome difficult life issues by being rooted in prayer and service to God, as did biblical women (Luke 8:1–4).

Each of us has powerful stories of overcoming boundaries of age, culture, economics, denomination, and so much more. Our victory is not in being free from the issues that life presents, but in our attitudes that testify to God's empowerment and grace. God is interceding for us. He is also refashioning, repairing, and altering us.

As God has spoken our world into existence, He upholds us by His mighty word (Hebrews 1:3). As we connect with Him and His promises in the Bible, we can hear and agree with His prayers for us. As we do, we have wisdom, comfort, joy, and more in this life, and faith in our eternal life.

While we can't prepare for all of life's events, we can rest in Christ's prayers for us, and awaken to His power at work in and through us.

— JOYCE DINKINS

Reflect

What's your testimony about God's prayers for you?

Where can you see His guidance in your life right now?

Do you believe God knows the issues that you face right now?

What can you share at this juncture with other women?

Faithful to Us

One day I started bawling my eyes out. I kept thinking about all the mistakes I made in the past. Even though I was a grown woman who was married, and the mother of three children, I kept thinking about how much I'd disappointed my parents. I'd only been a Christian a short time. I began to read the Scriptures, and over time, the Lord gave me several verses to hold onto.

Isaiah 54 told my life story. As I read it repeatedly, it ministered to me. God spoke these tender words of love to me on that sad day. Every verse seemed to have my name on it.

God became my husband. My prayer time became a lively, honest conversation between two good friends. I tell Him everything, and He talks back to me. Whenever I talk about this season of my life, when I took the Lord as my husband, I just begin crying. God has been so gracious to me. He's brought me through so much. He tenderly comforts me, again and again, through Isaiah's precious words.

—ANTONE HAYS

> *"For your Creator will be your husband; the LORD of Heaven's Armies is his name! He is your Redeemer, the Holy One of Israel, the God of all the earth."*
> (ISAIAH 54:5 NLT)

Leah is one of many women in Scripture who endured rejection and dishonor. The biblical description of her physical appearance does not sound inviting. To add insult to injury, her beautiful sister, Rachel, stood out as one of those sought-after women.

Leah's father, Laban, put her in the middle of an unfair love triangle. Jacob asked for Rachel's hand in marriage, and Laban agreed, but with the stipulation of Jacob working for Laban for seven years. After getting Jacob drunk at the wedding, Laban snuck Leah into the marriage bed, securing a marital union for his elder, undesirable daughter and for the younger, Rachel, the one Jacob wanted. The clueless groom found out about the deception the next morning. Laban used the excuse that his culture did not allow the younger sister to marry before the older. He allowed Jacob the promise of marrying Rachel but only after Jacob's promise to work for Laban another seven years (Genesis 29:21–26). Leah found herself in an awful situation. Her father arranged for her to marry a man who was in love with someone else.

I've never seen a verse in the Bible that said Jacob *finally* loved Leah. Not even after she gave him several children, or after her beautiful rival sister died. However, I found that there is a word describing Jacob's feeling toward Leah. He "hated" her—not in a malicious way, but he loved her *less* (Genesis 29:30).

Leah's father, husband, and sister all counted her out. They rejected her and did not value her; however, God loved Leah. He focused his attention on this unattractive, betrayed, rejected, and unwanted woman. *Jehovah Rapha*, "God our healer," turned these tragic events all the way around in Leah's life. "And when the LORD saw that Leah was hated, he opened her womb: but Rachel was barren" (Genesis 29:31). The verb *saw* is often used in Scripture before action on behalf of the oppressed and downtrodden (v. 31). God honored Leah, giving her high social status by allowing her to become a mother.

God wrapped his loving arms around Leah. I can't imagine the pain she suffered, alone in her tent while Jacob spent night after night with Rachel. Daily she had to look into his distant eyes as he passed her searching for Rachel. Yet, we see God rescued Leah out of this emotionally painful situation. Who wanted the ugly duckling? God did!

God opened Leah's physical womb, and he eventually unlocked her broken heart to himself. Initially, she recognized, *It's the Lord who has allowed me to have these sons.* She wanted to use them to draw her husband and win his affection (Genesis 29:32–34). But something happened when her fourth son was born. She named him *Judah*; this name meant praise. Leah said, "Now will I praise the LORD" (Genesis 29:35)!

Did Leah's circumstances change? Absolutely not. There's no evidence of an insensitive husband becoming faithful and loyal. Yet, something happened in Leah's heart. Her attention turned from her husband to the Lord, one who truly loved her. Leah moved from misery to praise of the Most High God.

God had conceived Leah before the beginning of the world. He had knit her together in her mother's womb, weak eyes and all. He saw all her days, which included the wedding-bed trick and the rejection by her husband. His perfect love embraced this woman and her dysfunctional family. God "saw" Leah, and finally, Leah "saw" God. She lifted her weak eyes to the One who knew her destiny.

Leah, whose son Levi became the original start of Israel's priestly tribe. Leah, whose fourth son, Judah, established the tribe Jesus was born out of. Leah, in the generational line of the mother of our Savior Jesus Christ. In God's providential timing, He took care of Leah.

Is God still God? Is He still able to do the same for the betrayed and rejected women in the world today? Jacob didn't come home and clearly state, "I've found another, and I'm moving on." Daily, Leah faced pushback in her own home by her mate. God extended grace beyond measure in her situation. Rachel had the eye of Leah's husband. Even though Leah had weak eyes, she had the eye of God Almighty!

Praise you, oh, Lord, that you are not like a man! Praise you, oh, Lord, that you have your eyes on those who are forgotten, or unlovely, or hated. Praise you that we are loved deeply by you even when those who are supposed to love us—don't. Praise you, Father, that you see us, and you say, "So shall the king greatly desire thy beauty: for he is thy Lord; and worship thou him" (Psalm 45:11).

— VICTORIA

Reflect

Recall a time when you've been betrayed, rejected, or mistreated.

What Scriptures did God use to remind you of His love and care?

In what ways can you share your experience with others who may be hurting?

Redeeming Our Shame

"My prayer journey, huh?" Mother threw her head back and started to laugh. "You want the nice-church-girl version? Or do you want the raw, ugly truth?"

I joined in her laughter, "Now, Mother, you know I want the truth, no matter how ugly." I eased back in my chair and looked at this dark-skinned, elderly woman. I'd only known her as a prayer warrior, who loved to encourage young people. "I know your testimony," I said, looking puzzled. "I didn't know there was a raw, ugly part."

"Well, fasten your seatbelt." She laughed again. "I'll try to give the short version.

"When I was ten . . . my older brother died suddenly. No one really wanted to talk about it, even though I was asking all kinds of questions. I cried hard those days in between his death and the day of the funeral. One of my aunts from out of town came into my room before she left. I was still crying even though the funeral had been over for hours. 'Listen, baby, you've got everybody worried with all this whooping and hollering you keep doing. They think you are going to get sick, like your brother, and something is going to happen to you. You've got to pull it together!' My aunt reached into her bag and pulled out a dirty white Bible with a zipper around it and her name engraved on the cover. She told me, 'I won this when I was a little girl in a Scripture memory verse contest. I'm giving it to you. Read a few verses every night before you go to sleep and ask God to talk to you and to comfort you. He will.' She pulled me close and hugged me tightly. 'I know how you feel.

I done lost a lot of people I cared about and loved. Sometimes it hurts for a long time. And sometimes the ache never goes away. But baby, you read this Bible, let God talk to you, and little by little you will feel better.'

"That was the beginning of my real prayer life. Before that, I'm sure I just said the blessing over my food and the Lord's Prayer before I went to bed each night. I didn't really think about what I was saying. But when I would read that dirty white Bible with the zipper around it, it did help. Later that year, when it was time for the young people to go up to the front of the church and spend time on the moaning bench, I was one of the first ones up there. This is the pew in the front of the church where people would sit until they were sure they had an encounter with Jesus. Mama told me it was the only way I could go to heaven and be with my brother if I died. Thank God, the preacher in that church knew how to make the salvation message plain. That year I asked Jesus into my heart.

"Years later, I went away to college. I'd never been in a big city before, and I really missed my family. But I did not dare tell my mother how badly I wanted to come home. She was so proud that one of her children was going to college, I had to finish.

"Then I met an upperclassman, an answer to my lonely nights. Mr. Love of My Life.

We met in the library the first week I was there. After the library closed, he invited me to his apartment to keep studying. That was the beginning. I spent the night, and I practically moved in for the rest of the school year. Well, after Christmas break, when I came back to school, I missed my first period."

Silence filled the room. Then Mother said, "You sure you want to hear all of this?"

I nodded my head, "If you want to tell me the whole story."

Mother took a deep breath. "Well, you know what's coming. I was pregnant. This was back in the day when abortions were cheap and right down the road. Nobody was protesting in front of the office, and nobody said that you were killing a baby. Mr. Love of My Life made all the arrangements. We didn't even talk about it. It was his last year of school, and he didn't want to get married. It was my first year of school, and how could I get through college with a baby? So, the next step seemed clear and practical. I found myself on a cold table going through an abortion procedure. I was ashamed to pray.

"By then I'd thrown that little dirty-white Bible to the side. I stopped reading the first night Mr. Love of My Life and I was together. How could I be having sex and praying to Jesus at the same time? I continued to go to church, and Mr. Love of My Life went with me, but we never talked about the inconsistencies in our walk with the Lord.

"Once again, even though we never talked about it, I assumed Mr. Love of My Life and I would continue our relationship even after he left school. But this is the crazy thing that happened. The night before he graduated, he had all his stuff packed up and ready to move out. He said to me, 'You can't be here when my parents come in the morning.' That made sense because I'm sure they didn't know we were sleeping together. So, I left, thinking I'd be included in the after-graduation dinner with his family, and that is when he'd introduce me as his girlfriend.

"Well . . ." Mother put her head back and closed her eyes as if she remembered it like it was yesterday. "His parents came and so did his girlfriend from his hometown."

"What?"

"You heard me, his girlfriend from home. He was living this double life with me the whole time. I was about to go over and make a fool of myself at his graduation when one of the other girls from the college, who knew him and knew we had been seeing each other, stopped me. 'I'm sorry to tell you like this. I thought Mr. Love of Your Life would have been man enough to tell you before today.'

"'Tell me what?' I was entirely in the dark.

"'That's his girlfriend over there, standing with his parents. She's from his hometown. I think they are engaged.'

"I watched for a while. I even got close enough to catch Mr. Love of My Life's eye. He never came over, and never said another word to me. I was devastated. I missed his graduation ceremony. I stayed in my room and cried my eyes out. I couldn't believe I had been such a fool. He never even called to apologize. I never saw him again.

"After that, I tried to pick up my Bible reading again for comfort, like I had after my brother died. But I felt so much shame. I felt like I'd let God down. I wanted to hide from Him, not run to Him. After that, I started drinking and partying hard on the weekends. I'd get my homework done during the week because

I was determined to finish college. But Friday and Saturday I was somewhere in the streets, wild.

"I found myself on that cold table down the street, not one more time, but three. By now my heart was so cold toward the Lord, I felt like I couldn't talk to Him at all. Oh, I still went to church, but my heart was far, far away from the Lord. As I got closer to graduation, I wanted things to change.

"After college, I found a job in a city not too far from my hometown. I asked the Lord for a new beginning. I started to attend a church there, and an older woman for some reason took an interest in me. She and her husband asked me over for lunch after church, and for some strange reason, I felt like I could tell her my story. My real story. She was like a grand-mother with one of those old-fashioned aprons that goes down almost hitting your ankles. When we'd talk, it was like she opened the apron and just let me vomit out my regrets, little by little.

"When I told her about the four abortions, she took me to Scripture and showed me the stories of David and of Paul. 'These men murdered,' she explained. 'Some argued that Paul wasn't a Christian and didn't know what he was doing. But David, on the other hand, when he murdered Bathsheba's hus-band, he knew full well what he was doing.'

"Then she took me to Psalm 51 and showed me David's prayer of repentance. She prayed with me several times until I realized in my heart God had forgiven me. The wall that had divided Jesus and me when I prayed no longer existed. I began to pray with such openness and honesty. I realized God did not turn His back on me; I turned my back on Him. His open arms never closed.

"The mother from the church also emphasized that both men were mightily used by God despite their decisions to take the life of another. She insisted God was going to use what I'd done in those college years for 'His glory and my good.'

"She was right. There is no way I could have the ministry I now have to help young people who are struggling in this area and many others. I tell them my story, and I've become the older woman with the open apron."

The Samaritan woman encountered Jesus at the well (John 4).

This woman did not go looking for Jesus; rather, He went looking for her. He told His disciples He had to go through Samaria (John 4:4). He had an appointment to see *this* woman on *this* day.

Jesus already knew this woman, inside and out. He saw her on the day she was conceived in her mother's womb, and He knew all about her activities up until that day. Yet, I have no doubt that His face, tone of voice, and words were filled with compassion.

On the other hand, she was immediately defensive and questioning. But the Master responded to her in love and kindness. Even when He exposed her living-with-a-man-now-not-her-husband issue, I don't hear a stern rebuke. Instead, I understand a gentle inquiry to let her know she was not talking to an ordinary man.

Jesus first asked her for water from the well, and He offered her himself—the Living Water. This encounter quenched a thirst within her. It so uplifted her that she forgot all about her reason for coming to the well at high noon to avoid the accusing eyes of people. She went running into town to tell people, "Come to meet a man." She had finally met a companion filled with forgiveness, gentleness, and compassion.

Before Jesus, the woman at the well got her water at noon. All the other women went for water in the morning, and their get-together was a social hour. The Samaritan woman never wanted to be a part of the well gathering; her shame was too great. However, after meeting and talking with Jesus, she unloaded her burden of guilt. She laced up her evangelistic running shoes and boldly went back into her hometown. She openly extended the invitation, "Come, see a man . . ." (John 4:29).

— A CHURCH MOTHER

Reflect

As you were reading, did God recall some areas of shame you need to bring to the cross of Christ?

Take a moment to pray with Him about it.

Review Psalm 51 slowly. Thank God for His cleansing as you specifically name troubling areas in your life.

Groaning for Us

I woke up this morning with my heart in my hands. Before I opened my eyes, her name was on my lips. I was doing so well these last couple of days. At this very moment, I am doing everything I can to keep from crying, to not be mad. But I am so hurt.

"Lord, I have not spoken with you in a while because I hurt so badly." Indeed, never have I experienced this type of engulfing pain. Yesterday someone asked me, "How many daughters do you have?" I said three, and then she asked their names. I took a deep breath and spoke their names. Later in the day, someone asked me, "How many kids do you have, how old are they, and where do they live?" I did not miss a beat. "I have three girls and a son, ages forty-two, thirty-eight, thirty-nine, and thirty-five," and then provided their locations.

But the reality is that the Lord took one of my daughters. It has been months.

Sunday is coming again. It was a Sunday that she left. It started off like most Sundays. I got up and prayed, studied the Sunday school lesson again, went to church, taught the lesson, did my worship thing, came home, fixed dinner, and parked my car for the night.

Someone called to tell me that my child had passed away. I thought, *I'm not sure why people lie so much. My baby is not gone. When I get there, it will all be a mistake.* Months later, it still feels like a mistake. But Christians will tell you that God does not make mistakes. As a matter of fact, someone said that exact thing to me yesterday. Yesterday was not a good day. This morning is starting off rough.

"Lord, I do not want to talk to you. Don't think that I am mad at you because I love you. But Lord, I'm so hurt, so broken, and I don't want to talk to you. You took my baby, my child."

I read, "He heals the brokenhearted and binds up their wounds" (Psalm 147:3 NIV). Her siblings are hurt, her Pops hurts, her children are hurt, and their dad is destroyed as well. How will he take care of four little children without her?

Sunday's coming again; it's both my son's and grandson's birthdays. We always do dinner, cake, and ice cream. We won't skip a beat.

"Lord, I am a fixer. I cannot fix this. Tears are at the corners of my eyes threatening to burst forward and engulf me in the depth of my sorrow. God, you see me. You are my El Roi, the God who sees me" (Genesis 16:13).

"I can hear you speak my name, but Lord, I do not want to talk to you. What do I say? I depend on you, Holy Spirit. 'We do not know what we ought to pray for, but the Spirit himself intercedes for us through wordless groans'" (Romans 8:26 NIV).

"What are you going to say to me?" I heard Him say, *I came into the world just for you; if you had been the only one, I still would have come for you.* "I have loved you with an everlasting love" (Jeremiah 31:3 NIV).

"Today is the first snowfall. As I walk outside, the sun has not come up yet, and the snow is still falling. As it touches my face, I realize how awed I am in your presence. I touch the wind chimes that bear my child's name (your child, Lord), and my heart aches to talk with you—my God, my Redeemer, the one who knows me, the one who sees me and loves me.

"Lord, you are my God and my *Jehovah Shalom*. You give me peace during this storm. I am weak today, and I need you to give me strength. I can't stop my tears from flowing; catch them and bring me joy."

—CONSTANCE ALBERTS

The fingers of my mind smoothed over the roughness of Constance's email. I'd asked her after reading this, "If you don't mind sharing, could you tell me what happened to your daughter?" I regret the question now, as she explained the painful journey of her last few years.

"Eight years ago, my two-year-old grandson accidentally shot himself in the head and died. My daughter grieved all those years. A month and a half ago they said she had a heart attack and died. Was it congestive heart failure—or did she die of a broken heart, shattered by the loss of her little boy?

"Eight months before my daughter's death, I had stood at the gravesite of my mother. Four months later, my birthday came. It happened to fall on a Sunday—Mother's Day."

NO PRAYER WORDS

I reread the email. *This can't be one person's life story for the last nine years. I'm certain Constance is my sister in Christ. How could our Father drop the ball; not once, but twice, and then again?*

I, too, want to pray, but I'm finding no words. Instead, I want to get my old, trusty walking shoes from the trunk of my car, lace them up, and hit the trail down by the lake. I wish to run fast and fierce until my lungs get that fiery burn, and I am bent over trying to catch my breath.

At the end of my exhausting exercise, I want Jesus to be there. Like a little girl burying her Afro'd head deep into her father's chest. But I refuse to ask for strength for another day's journey; instead, I beg God for it to be all over. So many stories like this one and so much pain.

"The creation groans." For days I've looked at Paul's words, "For we know that the whole creation groans and labors with birth pangs together until now" (Romans 8:22 NKJV). I've prayed, wondering *what's all this groaning about?* As I thought about Constance's pain, I also considered the trees outside my bedroom window.

During the twenty-five years I've lived here, I've watched the branches blow in each season. In the spring, they are draped in green buds, turning to full color all summer long. In the fall, I enjoy the various golden browns. I don't even mind the bare branches in winter because I know that in a short time, I'll see the buds reappear.

But for the last couple of years, the beautiful trees that uplifted my spirits as I turned the corner to my house have been dying. Some kind of disease has covered the leaves in black spots. The dark trunks are now covered with some sort of icky green stuff I'm afraid to touch. Now each summer, the city tree cutters take down several of the dying trees. Every now and then, I see a new, skinny, frail, baby tree planted. But it will be years before they grow tall enough for me to see them from my third-floor attic office window. The trees are groaning along with all of nature, and with us, for our original garden-of-Eden state, free of this earth's contamination, pollution, and pain.

GOD'S CHILDREN GROAN

Yes, I'll pray for Constance's family. I'll pray for that peace to descend on them that "surpasses all understanding" (Philippians 4:7 NKJV). Also, I'll use Constance's honesty to assist another brother or sister in Christ who is going through a similar experience. I'll pray that each of these family members will be strengthened in their inner man after their season of deep sorrow and their lamenting (see 2 Corinthians 1:16).

I'm waiting, crying, I want things to be put right. I long for the promised place with no more dying, no more tears (see Revelation 21:4).

A few months back, one of my friends and I got into it. Really. Yelling, the whole nine yards, a total misunderstanding. I was the guilty one. She attempted to express her disappointment with family members with a long history of hurtful actions towards her. She'd even shed more than a few tears as she talked about a relative—several, in fact, who use her like a filling station. They pump her for money and support but never give anything back. Not at Christmas, Easter, or Mother's Day. Not even on her birthday. She'd mailed card after card, stuffed with more than a couple of dollars. And sometimes the inconsiderate relative failed to acknowledge her generosity.

For some odd reason, out of character, I snapped. Maybe I was tired that day, or carrying some leftover anger from an argument I had had with my husband the night before. I didn't want to hear her temporary, seemingly unforgiving spirit. I wanted her to be the sacrificial lamb like Jesus: "Father, forgive them; for they know not what they do" (Luke 23:34). So instead of offering my compassion and a listening ear, I let her have it, the full force of my frustration.

I'm not sure what came out of my high tone of voice, but inwardly I was thinking, *just love the stupid fools. They don't know how to love, but you do! They probably will never change. They don't know how to improve. They are uncaring letches.*

She looked up at me, and I can still see her arms flailing, "This is why I just want to go home and be with the Lord; forget about all of this." She wanted to be with Jesus forever instead of here, dealing with me and everything else.

God's people, His creation, all call out for redemption. "I'm going to lay down my sword and shield, down by the riverside . . . to study war no more," wrote John Works in his Negro spiritual "Down by the Riverside." Somewhere in the deep-seated place in our hearts, we long to be with you, Jesus, at the Father's right hand, never to return to this world as we know it.

INTIMACY WITH THE HOLY SPIRIT

The Holy Spirit makes intercession for us, coming alongside us, assisting in all our ways—even when we are unaware of His presence. He is in our prayers and infirmities. He's groaning, sighing, and present in those problematic deep-down aching places. He experiences deep feelings that we cannot explain or express. He is on the inside of the intense anxiety that exists in the oppressed and burdened heart of the Christian.

No words are released. There are no words; no one can dare ascribe a language to describe the depths of the sorrow. The Holy Spirit comes alongside us and holds us up. He is that much-needed support and sustaining power. It's His covering that enables one to lift the head off the pillow, lift one foot before the other, and move forward when there seems to be an army within pulling in the opposite direction. Also, like Christ, He's bilingual. He's expressing the human heart and able to communicate it to the Lord, shaping it into a form that fits the Father's desire and will.

— VICTORIA

Reflect

Recall a time when you may have deeply desired for all of this earthly activity to be completed.

How did you see God's plan of redemption fitting in?

How can we help those in the valley understand the Holy Spirit's comfort and help?

Deep Diving with Us

I used to fear deep water. I almost drowned, or at least that's how it seemed in my eleven-year-old mind. I was right at the edge of the pool when I started to bob and gasp for air. It seemed like forever until the lifeguard extended that metal hook to me. No more deep water for me after that. Of course, I had lots of company on the sidelines.

Christians are called to "deep water." Something happens when we have submerged in Christ's life: a cleansing, a renewing, and a resurrection. It is through this baptism that we die to the old and rise to new life in Christ. We must be baptized in the Spirit—submerged completely and utterly. "For John truly baptized with water; but ye shall be baptized with the Holy Ghost not many days hence" (Acts 1:5). No more touching the bottom and far away from the sides of the pool. No shoreline to cling onto, entirely at the mercy of the water, being carried by the current of God to whomever or wherever God decides.

A camp counselor took me out of the kiddie pool, telling me that I was too big to be with the little ones. She taught me how to swim in a man-made lake with sloping sides and a depth of twenty feet. She was an excellent counselor. Eventually, I became a junior lifesaver! To pass the test, we had to rescue a person struggling in deep water. "Whatever you do," the instructor bellowed, "don't stay on the surface of the water as you approach the drowning person!" We were told that one could not save a drowning person by remaining on the surface. When a drowning person sees the rescue swimmer, they will try to lift their body up by pushing the rescuer's head under the water. If the rescuer stays on the surface, the drowning person will drown the rescuer. We were taught to dive deep as we approached the drowning person and swim around, so we could grab them from behind and swim with them back to shore.

Perhaps it is time for more of us to go deeper into the Holy Spirit. People don't need platitudes, overly used words, and common religious clichés. Platitudes lack power! "But ye shall receive power, after that the Holy Ghost is come upon you: and ye shall be witnesses unto me both in Jerusalem, and in all Judaea, and in Samaria, and unto the uttermost part of the earth" (Acts 1:8).

So many are drowning—in sin, hopelessness, desperation, and fear—but "surface-swimming" Christians cannot save them. Spiritless swimmers may find themselves pushed under the water by those who need rescue. But those who have been baptized in Christ's Holy Spirit have the power to pray for and witness to those in deep trouble—those who need the saving love of Jesus. Now I challenge you, my brothers and sisters, come on, let's go into the deep.

GETTING TO KNOW JESUS

As a struggling and emotionally confused college student, I did not know God cared about my personal pain. I cried out, but mostly to myself. The political dogma of the day declared that religion was the opiate of the masses. As a result, I viewed my God as distant, inaccessible, and cold. I was amazed to know later that God was there all the time.

I had grown up going to church, but I did not really know Jesus personally. I couldn't comprehend that deity and friendship could go together. After I left home for the strange world of Massachusetts, I was left with neither a church home nor a relationship with Jesus to carry me through. The darkness of disconnection from God settled in, and my decision-making was influenced by my own limited thinking. I partied rather than studied; I protested rather than attended class; I sought boyfriends instead of the lover of my soul. I was like Mary Magdalene, looking for love and life in all the wrong places.

THE SEARCH

Mary Magdalene and the women came to the tomb looking for Jesus. They had come to anoint his body and prepare it for a proper burial. How shocked they must have been to discover an empty tomb! In John's version of this story, Mary cries out, "We don't know where they have taken him." It seemed that the world was always trying to take away our Jesus, to rob Him of His power and divinity. My college awareness of the gross inequities of racism and imperialism seemed to have stolen any hope in the Sunday school and God I had met as a child. Yet the search for God will carry us away from places of death and destruction.

"'Why do you look for the living among the dead? He is not here" (Luke 24:5–6 NIV). And the women turned in another direction. Their assignment had been changed, from burying a body to proclaiming a risen Savior. These women were the very first evangelists, and they announced to the men that Jesus lives! Hallelujah.

Finally, I met Jesus after college. I got to know Him as I moved back to Detroit and began spending mornings on my knees. My time shifted from petition to worship. It dawned on me that death could never take Him away. In fact, nothing could. He lived, and so did I. Just like the women at the tomb, I, too, turned in another direction and rededicated my life to Christ.

Not long afterward, I cried tears of joy in a small Tanzanian village as pastors and intercessors prayed for the safe return of the mission group with which I traveled. Hands were laid upon us, and oil was poured to anoint us. In the Bible, this anointing signified God's servant being set apart for God's use. All I felt was love. I was so far away from my home, yet I had found a home in the Living God. Like the women at the tomb, God changed my assignment and sent me out to tell others about the Lord.

— GEORGIA HILL

Teaching Us to Pray

When I started to learn how to pray, I did not know about the Holy Spirit's help. I just remembered hearing long, involved prayers in church—prayers filled with *thee* and *thou*, with all kinds of long, high-sounding titles for God.

Each night I lay on my bed thinking about all the prayers I had heard. *Now, which one impressed God the most?* I thought. Or, *who would I try to sound like when I say my prayers?* I'd turn the thoughts repeatedly in my mind. *Did God like the prayers with the big important-sounding words?* I must admit I had no idea what those spiritual phrases meant, but I'd be willing to repeat them if that's what God wanted.

I wondered if I needed to say the commands that beat up on the devil. *No, I'd think, I need to sing with a deep holy voice. Or maybe God likes the soft whispery voices. No*, I'd argue with myself, *that can't be it; everyone knows that the loudest voices get the most response.* I'd fall to sleep thinking about my favorite impressive title for God, *Oh Thou Most High and Holy God.* I'd use that one tomorrow. During all this back and forth, I spent no time in prayer.

At some point, I started thinking my prayers. This was wonderful for me because there were no words to get just right. For a while, I thoroughly enjoyed these kinds of prayers. I'd arrange the words in my head until I thought it all sounded good. No prayers ever escaped my lips.

One day, I read the passage about Jesus instructing His disciples, giving them a model for prayer:

> *"When ye pray, say, Our Father which art in heaven, Hallowed be thy name. Thy kingdom come. Thy will be done, as in heaven, so in earth. Give us day by day our daily bread. And forgive us our sins; for we also forgive every one that is indebted to us. And lead us not into temptation; but deliver us from evil."*
> (Luke 11:2–4)

Wow, the first thing that gripped my attention was that Jesus's twelve disciples and I had the same problem. We all had the questions of: how do I pray, what do I say, and what do I call God? Jesus gave them the uncomplicated answer without rebukes. He taught a simple prayer.

I couldn't wait to kneel by my bed and open my mouth and call God "Our Father." That was just the beginning of an intimate time of sharing my heart, my mind, my day, and my life with the Lord.

I wonder how many new Christians find that they have this problem and are wondering about the proper way to pray. I found that the Lord never rebukes us when we seek Him sincerely. He waits for us to turn to Him when we don't know what to do or how to do it. Our Father teaches us to pray; His Spirit teaches us how to pray.

— MOTHER ADELL DICKERSON

Reflect

Write out what you believe it looks like for you to "go deeper" with the Holy Spirit in prayer.

Add how you think it would benefit others too.

Read Acts 1:8. What does this passage say to you, and how can you accomplish this in this day and time?

Blessed
IN OUR STRUGGLES

JESUS CARRIED ME

A new heart also will I give you, and a new spirit will I put within you: and I will take away the stony heart out of your flesh, and I will give you an heart of flesh. And I will put my spirit within you. (Ezekiel 36:26–27)

My prayer journey started with fire; I burned my ex-boyfriend's clothes and landed in jail for three weeks. I was in my twenties, a single parent with a daughter about age five. The daycare worker kept her while I was in jail. I cried and prayed the entire time. The lawyers kept telling me I'd get serious prison time. A nun would come to the jail every day, encouraging and praying with me. God protected me.

When I went before the judge, she said, "I think you need therapy, not jail time." She gave me five years probation. I followed her advice and got counseling. That's when I started talking about the sexual abuse I had suffered as a child.

I couldn't pray at home. There was an evil presence. I'd be afraid to pray, and had stopped altogether. Then this woman invited me to her prayer and Bible study group. They prayed over me until I was able to pray at home by myself. My personal prayer time is much better now. It's evident Jesus carried me through; He was praying for me when I didn't know how or what to pray for myself. He still prays for me.

—TINA PAYNE

God Knows Our Desperation

Have you ever been desperate? I don't mean inconvenienced, a little concerned, or having a day where things didn't go as you had planned or hoped. I mean *desperate*. As in, *I don't know how I'm going to survive this . . . this is hopeless . . . there is no way* (you fill in the blank), or, *Jesus, I need you now—not an hour from now, not a minute from now, but right now!* I have experienced that type of desperation a few times in my life. Each time, I was fearful for my life. Perhaps the time that I despaired the most was when I literally could not breathe.

My doctor said it was an acute case of bronchitis, but I knew my inability to breathe was an outward, physical sign of the toxic environment I found myself in at work.

Often tearfully saying, "This isn't what I signed up for," I hated going to my place of employment because of the drama. This went on for months. Then one day a close friend asked me how I was doing. I wept as I answered, and it became difficult to breathe. This was not a panic attack because I was not panicked. Instead, I was *desperate*.

Each breath became a struggle. With each battle to take the next breath, I would say to myself, *I can't continue like this.* But that admission was quickly followed by, *I cannot skip out on work. What will people say? I have too many responsibilities.*

When my doctor prescribed an inhaler for me and told me to stay in bed, it was an answer to my desperate cries. I didn't go to work, church, or anywhere else.

When people called to say that they wanted to come by and pray for me, I told them, "No." If they prayed for me and laid hands on me, I would get better. At that point, I didn't want to get well. I had an excuse for hiding away. After all, I was obeying my doctor's orders. He instructed me to stay in bed until I was no longer struggling to breathe. My friends, my husband, and church members had no idea how desperate I was, but God did. The Lord understood my deepest need. He ministered to me for over a month, meeting with me right there in my bedroom. He brought me through one of the darkest times of my life. Even though I could not pray for myself and I did not allow people to come to my house to pray over me, Jesus, the great Intercessor, prayed over me.

TIMES OF DESPERATION

Our times of desperation may not always take our breath away, but we will have I-can't-live-like-this-anymore moments. It happens to all of us. Our first instinct may be to run. We can, but we will not get far. We cannot outrun God.

A young Egyptian slave girl on the run, Hagar was running away from her owner and mistress Sarai (Genesis 16). Hagar was pregnant by her master, Abram, Sarai's husband. Sarai had given Hagar to Abram in hopes that she would conceive the child God had promised Abram and Sarai. Hagar did conceive, and began to despise her mistress Sarai.

When Sarai complained to Abram about how miserable she felt, he told her to do what she wanted to Hagar. Sarai mistreated Hagar so severely, she ran away, likely fearing for her life and that of her unborn child. Hagar was desperate.

How could someone she served faithfully for ten years punish her for doing what she had been ordered to do by Sarai, who gave her to Abram? Her young body did what Sarai's could not, and Sarai felt threatened. Hagar ran for the desert.

When Hagar stopped running long enough to rest and drink from a spring, an angel of the Lord met her: "Hagar, Sarai's servant, where have you come from, and where are you going?" (Genesis 16:8 NLT). This angelic representative of God called her by name and named her crisis. She replied, "I'm running away from my mistress, Sarai" (V. 8 NLT). What the angel says next is at first jarring. The angel tells Hagar to go back to Sarai and submit to her. *Wait. A. Minute.*

Yes, go back to Sarai, with a promise that all will be well in the end. The angel added, "I will give you more descendants than you can count" (V. 10 NLT). The angel tells Hagar that the Lord has heard her cries and has heard her misery. The angel tells her that she will have a son and tells her of the great plans that God has for her son. Hagar returns to Sarai, but not before she gives a name to the Lord who spoke to her, *El Roi:* "you are the God who sees me" (V. 13 NLT). Hagar is the first person in the Bible to give God a name.

Hagar returned to Sarai. We don't know whether Sarai treated Hagar better, but we do know Hagar knew that God saw her and protected her. God promised she would give birth to a son, who would lead a nation. Because God saw her, Hagar was no longer desperate. The slave girl gave birth to Ishmael. This runaway resolutely put her trust in the promise and the process of an all-seeing and all-knowing God.

DESPERATE PEOPLE DO DESPERATE THINGS

When we're desperate, we might do things that seem rash—like asking people not to pray. A desperate person may put up with indignities that a non-desperate person would never stand for, like the Canaanite woman we read about in the Gospels (Matthew 15:21–28).

As Jesus was on his way to Tyre and Sidon, a woman approached Him and cried out, "Have mercy on me, O Lord, Son of David! For my daughter is possessed by a demon that torments her severely" (Matthew 15:22 NLT). Jesus refused to respond to her cries verbally. Despite His silence, the Canaanite woman continued to follow Jesus and cried out for Him to help her daughter (VV. 23–25).

Jesus's disciples told Jesus to send her away because she kept crying out. Desperate people do desperate things. Then, in what appeared to be Jesus honoring the requests of the disciples and not the cries of a desperate Gentile woman, Jesus told the Canaanite, "It isn't right to take food from the children and throw it to the dogs" (V. 26 NLT).

Wait. A. Minute. Did Jesus call her a *dog*? She responded, "That's true, Lord, but even dogs are allowed to eat the scraps that fall beneath their masters' table" (V. 27 NLT). Jesus responded, "Your faith is great. Your request is granted" (V. 28 NLT). Her daughter was healed as soon as Jesus stated her request had been granted.

The Canaanite woman knew that with just a word, Jesus could heal her daughter. This mother didn't care about the process. All she wanted was a promised outcome of deliverance.

Like Hagar, the Canaanite woman was willing to suffer through a debasing set of circumstances to grasp promises spoken by God, who saw her desperate situation.

Like Hagar, the Canaanite knew she didn't have the power to change her situation. She had no right to ask Jesus for anything; she was not the right ethnicity, didn't have wealth, and she wasn't married to a high-ranking government official. She had nothing, but *great faith*—assurance that Jesus could heal her daughter and a conviction that she would do whatever it took to get an answer to her cries (vv. 27–28).

The Canaanite woman was desperate. God, Jesus, saw her desperation, and in the process reminded us all that God sees us in our despair. God will move on our behalf, God guides us through a process to get to His promises.

Us, the ones who are called by His name, who have asked Jesus to be our Lord and Savior. He came to us, the ones who have access to His very throne of grace, the ones He promised never to leave or forsake.

TRUSTING GOD

We know when we are desperate. Still, it's sometimes hard to be honest with God about how much our circumstances are stressing us. It's sometimes hard to be honest with ourselves about how huge our concerns and burdens are. "Put your big-girl panties on and deal with it," some say. We have bought into the lie that since we got ourselves into a mess, we need to get ourselves out. We put on a superhero cape, but do not want to admit that it is just for show. The reality is we are desperate, and want nobody to know how bad things are inside our home, our body, our church—all our broken places. We forget that God invites us to cast all our cares on Him so that He can carry the heavy load for us and give us rest. We forget that Jesus is our Intercessor when all we have are tears and a groan. That God invites us to bring everything to Him. He already has beautiful plans for our lives (Psalm 40:5). God's hope-filled promises don't mean we will not face circumstances that break us, hurt us. God does allow situations that drive us to tears and leave us gasping. When we experience these things, and we will, it does not mean God doesn't love us, or that we have weak faith. God is aware of our desperation and does not leave us alone; He sees our tears, hears our cries, and remains *with* us.

God doesn't promise immediate deliverance from every situation. The angel of the Lord told Hagar to go back to Sarai. *But I thought that God said He would not put more on us than we can bear,* you might be thinking to yourself. Well, God did not say that. Besides, when we say something like that, we're making getting through our problems about "our strength," and not leaning on God's. We interpret our mounting problems (or someone else's) through the lens of how strong *we* are, rather than on how God's strength is made perfect in our weakness (2 Corinthians 12:9; Matthew 11:28–30).

We tell ourselves, *no need to bother God with this. He won't put more on me than I can bear. I got this.* He has promised, "And God shall wipe away all tears from their eyes; and there shall be no more death, neither sorrow, nor crying, neither shall there be any more pain: for the former things are passed away"

(Revelation 21:4). However, my sisters, He does not promise that day will be tomorrow.

Trust God.

So, what to do in our desperate moments? Stand on what God has to say in the Scriptures. He tells us that as He was with Hagar, He will be with us in every situation—even our desperate situations.

> *"So be strong and courageous! Do not be afraid and do not panic before them. For the LORD your God will personally go ahead of you. He will neither fail you nor abandon you."* (DEUTERONOMY 31:6 NLT)

> *The faithful love of the LORD never ends! His mercies never cease. Great is his faithfulness; his mercies begin afresh each morning. I say to myself, "The LORD is my inheritance; therefore, I will hope in him!" The LORD is good to those who depend on him, to those who search for him. So, it is good to wait quietly for salvation from the LORD.* (LAMENTATIONS 3:22–26 NLT)

In those desperate times of life, we need to be like Hagar and the Canaanite woman. We need to let our tears be our prayers, be honest about our wounds, tell God about what is breaking our heart, and report to Him concerning the people who are hurting us. *But doesn't God already know?* you may be asking. Yes, God knows; however, by telling God about our desperate situations, we are telling God that we trust Him with the broken places of our lives. We are confessing, "Lord, I can't fix this. I need you to help a sister out."

Many times, when we tell God how badly it hurts, God tells us that His grace is sufficient (2 Corinthians 12:9). When that happens, it does not mean that He does not know how desperate we are. God knows. He is seeing if we are willing to trust Him. He is providing an opportunity to trust Him through a process that aligns with His perfect will. Sometimes we need to go through seasons of desperation to get to the fulfillment of God's promises. As we begin to trust God for the hope of bringing us through our seasons of misery, we find that His grace really is enough. The more we trust God with our burdens, the more room we give God to do all the heavy lifting of answering prayer.

—MICHELLE LOYD-PAIGE

Reflect

Describe a time when you have been desperate.

How did God come to your rescue?

What do we learn about God in desperate situations?

God Waits with Us

I waited twenty-seven years for God to answer my first prayer request. I was only three years old when I began to pray that prayer. Year after year, I wanted God to say yes but He said wait. Wait? Why did I have to wait? I was merely asking God to do something He already promised in His Word to do. Regardless of that truth, I still had to wait.

I waited twenty-seven years for my dad to surrender his life to Christ. He had accepted Christ at one point. He tried to live differently on several other occasions, but the real, lasting change came after he was diagnosed with Stage 4 lung cancer. He ultimately surrendered to God when he was in remission a year after his diagnosis. He lived for a total of five years after remission.

Waiting is an inevitable part of life. However, we don't accept that notion as readily today, because instant gratification has become a part of our daily lives. Long gone are the days of waiting for phone lines to be free, vacation photos to be developed, and important messages to arrive in the mail. We can access almost anything we want or need with a simple click, swipe, or tap on our smartphone or laptop.

If an item is unavailable for our immediate purchase, we won't order the item and wait for it to arrive. Instead, we'll shop around until we find it. And if we have no other choice but to place an order, we pay top dollar for expedited shipping. No wonder we wrestle with waiting; we're so accustomed to getting everything we want exactly when we want it. That's the way of this world.

God's way is different, and we should be careful not to treat Him like a local retailer. We can't check out God's "competitors" to see if they have what we want when God tells us what we want is currently unavailable. As believers, we can approach waiting on God as a spiritual development process. He will help us to appropriately respond when we must wait.

Mary's, Martha's, and Hannah's prayer requests help us examine our responses when God tells us, *wait*.

Waiting for healing. When Lazarus's health dramatically declined, Lazarus's sisters Mary and Martha sent word to Jesus, who was close to them and Lazarus (John 11:3). But Jesus wasn't nearby. Surely, Jesus could have reached Lazarus quickly with supernatural power, but he didn't. Jesus did not even set out to Lazarus for two extra days. When he arrived, Mary and Martha were relieved to see Him, but they had been expecting Him to show up in time to heal Lazarus (John 11:21, 32). Through tears of His own, Jesus headed toward Lazarus's tomb and raised Lazarus from the dead (John 11:11–13). If Jesus could resurrect Lazarus, why did He not heal Lazarus before he died? Why wait?

Jesus waited until all the parts of God's plan came together. The two-day journey and four-day death add necessary complexity to the story so that everyone would "really believe" (John 11:14). The mixed crowd of believers and unbelievers not only witnessed an undeniable miracle but also gave glory to God alone. Waiting for Jesus allowed Mary and Martha to experience God's complete authority over death and life.

Waiting to birth life. Hannah had had enough of Peninnah, the other woman in her blended marriage. Polygamy was customary in their day, but this family unit was not a model one.

Peninnah's kids were not only painful reminders that Hannah could not have any children; her constant insults to Hannah caused deep emotional and physical stress. She was surrounded in family drama. Elkanah's words and actions brought Hannah no comfort (1 Samuel 1:7–8). A woman's worth was determined by her ability to have children; thus, Hannah felt empty and flawed. Nothing would have been as valuable to her as having a child, a son.

With a heavy heart, desperate and crying out to God for a son, she promised to dedicate her son to God's full-time ministry. In faith. And then Hannah's wait was over, finally. Her womb opened, and she gave birth to Samuel—and she kept her promise to God.

We don't know for sure, but the prayer we read in the Bible was probably not Hannah's first. I imagine her initial prayers might have focused on image, self-worth, comparisons to Peninnah, and concern for what others were saying about her. However, the prayer we read in the Bible had a changed focus.

Driven by hopelessness and years of waiting, Hannah looked up, to God's glory and mission. The son she so desperately wanted, that would have validated her as a woman, became her willing sacrifice surrendered to God.

While Hannah was waiting for God to answer her prayer, perhaps He was waiting for her to say the *right* prayer. We don't know that, and yes, many encourage us to pray for whatever we want. Yet, as Christian believers, our prayers are to have the right motives. What happens when we pray with the right motives, and God still says *wait*? Although waiting can be challenging, we can trust our requests to our all-knowing God. He gives us what we need to wait.

RESPONDING WHEN GOD SAYS WAIT

Waiting on God requires action. In their book, *Disciplines of the Holy Spirit*, Siang-Yang Tan and Douglas H. Gregg encourage us to persevere when we want to give up (Luke 18:1), when mountain-sized obstacles seem overwhelming (Mark 11:23–24), and when we don't receive a quick answer from God. Xochitl Dixon's book, *Waiting for God: Trusting Daily in God's Plan and Pace,* provides many insights about the blessings we experience in the wait.

Waiting on God can raise our expectations for our situations to change. We can expect God not only to answer the request we've made but also to answer requests we haven't thought to ask (Ephesians 3:20).

The Bible gives us many examples of the results of waiting on God. Waiting:

- Increases our faith; Noah waited for rain. See Genesis 6.
- Fuels our hope; Simeon waited for the Messiah. See Luke 2.
- Calls for obedience; Jesus waited to start His ministry. See Luke 2.
- Reminds us to listen; Abraham waited for a sacrifice. See Genesis 22.

- Takes perseverance; Moses waited in the wilderness. See Exodus 13.
- Challenges us to trust; Job waited to be restored. See Job 3.
- Shows respect for God; Hebrew boys waited in a fiery furnace. See Daniel 3.
- Moves us to surrender; Ruth waited for a husband. See Ruth 3.
- Inspires praise and worship; Paul and Silas waited in chains. See Acts 16.
- Promotes silence and solitude; Daniel waited in the lions' den. See Daniel 6.
- Keeps us focused on God-given dreams and visions. See Genesis 40.

Scripture clearly illustrates that God will sometimes tell us to wait and that we should be ready to respond with a biblical mindset. Examples from the lives of Mary, Martha, Hannah, and many others offer us additional insight into having the right responses to waiting.

Expect Jesus to come, as Mary and Martha did as they waited to see Jesus; they didn't doubt He would come. When He finally arrived, they ran to Him. They weren't surprised to see Him; they only questioned His timing. As we wait on God to answer our prayers, we must remember that His timing, thoughts, and ways are not like ours (Isaiah 55:8–9; 2 Peter 3:8).

Checking our motives is essential. Hannah was overwhelmed by the thought of not being a mother and envied Peninnah. God doesn't want us to have a horizontal view of our lives. When we do, we see only what others around us have, and that limits our expectations. He wants us to have a vertical view: while we wait, we can look to Jesus, who initiates and perfects our faith (see Hebrews 12:2).

Let's partner with God, author our own stories of waiting on Him, and join the biblical cast of believers who don't merely wait on God, but wait with high expectations.

— ERICKA LOYNES

Reflect

What are you waiting for?

What are your motives, and your expectations?

Waiting Is an Invitation

We all receive invitations, for birthday parties, bridal or baby showers, retirement celebrations, or a simple lunch with a friend. What do we do when we get invited? We check our schedules for conflicting appointments to determine whether it's a good day to attend and what to reschedule. When it comes to ministry engagements, we may look at the schedule and pray to ask God if the invitation is something He would like us to accept or decline.

Not all invitations are to be accepted. Similarly, some are not to be declined. Prayer helps us to hear God's thoughts above our own and nudges us to act. The hardest part, however, is when God is not quick to show us if the answer is yay or nay. So we wait.

Waiting is proactive; it's an invitation to trust, though we don't typically enjoy waiting. It's a necessary part of growth in trusting God.

For years I rushed into God's presence and shared all of my thoughts and desires and hoped God would say yes to everything I prayed for. I had to grow in my prayer life and come to see that God welcomes me to talk to Him and invites me to listen.

How is God inviting you to wait in prayer? Is your prayer life a monologue or a dialogue?

What's your most memorable invitation? My most memorable invitations have been to become a student at various colleges and to become a part of ministry teaching teams or church staffs. Invitations that have blown my mind have been to become my husband's marriage partner, to share in distinguished conferences as a speaker, and to be an author.

Invitations in life humble us, affirm or redirect, and include us in God's plan. So does the invitation to pray.

In recent years I have prayed and waited on God to restore my health and my husband's health and to grant peace in all circumstances. I've also been directed by God to uplift communities that are in need and waited on Him to share the best way to give to these communities. I have waited for writing opportunities, like this project that you are reading now.

I stand amazed at the timetable of God.

In Mark 5:21–42, we see Jairus relying on God's power and trusting in new ways, and we see God's power released not only in Jairus's life, but in his daughter's life, and in the life of the woman with the issue of blood.

Prayer accomplishes several things; it:

- Stretches our faith muscles.
- Ensures that we rely on God and not on our own understanding, timeline, and power.
- Reminds us that God is sovereign and we are not.

Are you trusting the God of all creation or in your own sufficiency? Scripture on prayer that empowers me to trust God more: "This is the confidence we have in approaching God: that if we ask anything according to his will, he hears us" (1 John 5:14 NIV).

Prayer reminds us that God hears: "And if we know that he hears us—whatever we ask—we know that we have what we asked of him" (1 John 5:15 NIV). Prayer reminds us that God will answer our requests. Prayer and waiting in prayer remind me that:

God is sovereign and I am not.

God is perfect and I am not.

I am needy for God and His direction and not the other way around.

God's yes and no can be trusted and will be for my good and His glory.

The "God-ness" of God is never diluted in my waiting and neither is His call on my life watered down when He doesn't answer quickly.

— COKIESHA BAILEY ROBINSON

Reflect

How is God inviting you to trust Him?

What prayers are you waiting for God to answer?

What stops you from accepting His answer to your prayers?

Are you willing to pray, trust, wait, and act?

God Heals Us

I had just completed sitting for the State Bar of Texas. The night before the essay portion of the exam, I was so nauseous. *Why?* I thought. The most intimidating part of the exam had already passed; the next day of this three-day exam was the essay portion—my strong area—so I thought, *I can't possibly be that nervous about the test.* After talking briefly with my husband about the perplexing situation as we sat in a pharmacy parking lot, he asked, "You don't think you're pregnant, do you?" That was absolutely the *furthest* thing from my mind. Once I began breathing again, I replied, "Don't know, but we are not going to find out tonight!" I figured, *if I'm pregnant, I'll still be pregnant after the essay portion of the exam.* Sure enough, the day after the exam, we took a pregnancy test, and it was positive.

About sixteen weeks later, we had our first sonogram to check on the baby's development. That's when our lives forever changed. The doctors diagnosed our daughter with hypoplastic left heart syndrome—a rare and severe congenital heart defect. For all functional purposes, it was as if our baby had half a heart. She would need open-heart surgery at birth.

Four days after birth, our daughter had heart surgery. And again at six months old. And another surgery would occur at three or four years.

Thus began our season of various periods of waiting. I waited for my baby's delivery, uncertain of what the outcome would be. During her first surgery, which was several hours, I waited. During her twenty-one days in the hospital following her delivery and operation, I waited. In the days that followed, as our family walked through God's healing process for her, I waited. We all waited.

HOW MUCH MORE?

Our waiting seasons can be some of the most frustrating, agonizing, debilitating, terrifying, and downright infuriating times. They are the times when our *What's to come, Lord?* seems to hang in perpetuity. We may find ourselves questioning, *Lord, did I hear you correctly? Lord, why did you put this desire in me, if it will never be met? Lord, when is my change going to come? How long, Lord; how much more of this suffering can I take?*

These are times that we can become spiritually constipated. Mentally stuck. That's right—much like being physically slowed. That's our spiritual condition when we have a backup of emotions that are unacknowledged and unreleased. Emotions can stagnate, harden, block, and hinder. Hinder spiritual movement—blocking God's Spirit that provides the enlightenment, encouragement, peace, strength, and so much more we need during our waiting periods.

God wants us to get real. Often there is the expectation that the Christian's response to "How are you doing?" should be "I'm blessed and highly favored." In my waiting seasons (and with the help of a wonderfully anointed therapist), I learned that I had to *allow* myself to recognize my emotions. I did not have to stay in the emotion, but I at least needed to confess: "I'm angry, worried, afraid, discouraged, frustrated, insecure . . . exhausted." When we genuinely admit the difficulty of the season, we experience the most growth. You name it, and then allow it to pass.

As I struggled to figure out what it looked like for a believer to go through periods of waiting, I learned to do three things to help navigate those tough times. First, acknowledge what is. Be truthful about the circumstances. This idea that a person lacks faith if she tells the truth concerning the facts of her situation is a lie from the enemy. Whenever we encounter Jesus performing miracles, the Scriptures are very clear about the factual things. In fact, the details and clarity about the conditions are what amplify the magnitude of the miracle! Failure to be honest and genuine about where we are diminishes the effectiveness of our witness to God's power, and may even cause us to appear delusional or naïve to others. It also keeps us from living well.

Suppression of real and valid emotions can lead to several mental and physical health challenges that only grow worse with time. Finally, suppressing emotions prevents us from fully realizing God's power. Unless we recognize the depth of the low, we cannot fully appreciate the length to which God's love goes to reclaim us, and the power of God's love to renew and restore us.

Second, let go. We can relinquish the phrase *should be*. It's difficult to see God in our experiences when we refuse to look at our experience authentically. Instead, we often affix our gaze, our mind, and our heart on what we think life should be. With every *should be,* we construct a fragile, two-dimensional framework of a house of finite materials. We close ourselves off from the infinite wisdom and power of a holy, loving God whose heart's desire is to see His children blessed. We resign ourselves to shallow living. While focusing on *should be*, we miss what *is*, how God *is* present and moving in our circumstances, and the miracle of God's sustaining power through it all.

Then, in a behavioral modification process, when we let go of something, we must replace what is released with something else. Otherwise, human nature is to cling to what is known and what is familiar. After acknowledging what *is* and relinquishing what *should be*, we adhere to the truth of God's Word concerning what *can be*. God wants us to have abundant life (John 10:10). God never promised that everything we experience is going to feel good. However, He does promise "all things work together for good to them that love God" (Romans 8:28). It is not our role to determine how this abundant life is going to manifest, or how a situation is going to work together for our good, or what God's plans for our lives may be. Our only role is to be open and look for where God is present in it all. Because despite what we are experiencing, He is still *Emmanuel*, God who is with us.

Failing to face the truth about what *is* causes us to be full of compacted emotions. Fixating on what *should be* further solidifies our already compacted feelings. And rejecting the truth and power of God's Word leaves us dry—ripe for spiritual shutdown. That makes it difficult to pray, see hope, hear God, or feel God's presence; instead, focused on our problems and circumstances, we are so disgruntled and angry with God that we can't even bring ourselves to turn in the direction of the throne room, much less enter in and be vulnerable before the Lord.

The Father knows what we are going through. The question is whether we will allow ourselves to acknowledge God's presence and let God give us the power we need to learn and grow through our waiting season. Yes, God had us in His waiting room several times concerning our daughter. I rejoice to report she is a healthy preteen. God is truly amazing.

— YULISE WATERS

Reflect

What does spiritual constipation look like in your life?

Is there anything you need to let go of?

Read Romans 8:28 and take time to pray for yourself and others God may bring to mind.

Laying Burdens Down

It was around 2:00 a.m. when the phone call came. The call that no one asks for or waits for, but has happened nonetheless, sending a shockwave throughout the entire community of believers. Our pastor had a sudden heart attack, and sadly, he passed away.

Bad news affects people differently. This unexpected report started a rapid dissension and ignited a spiral of emotions. For many, the passing of their beloved pastor and friend created an unhealthy lament. It opened a wound that should have been treated with the medicine of the Holy Spirit. Instead, it resulted in anger, bitterness, and pain. A service was organized to allow a time of open grief. A gathering at the altar to pray for heart-healing.

Sadly, instead of seeing this as an occasion for healing, many people questioned, argued, and even tried to stop this prayer service! It became more apparent as the date approached that several in the congregation were angry with God. "He took away our leader." They questioned, "Why should I seek the One who is responsible for this unfortunate situation? Why would I entrust my heartache and pain to the One who should have protected or kept safe the one we loved?" They felt abandoned by God. They refused to let the sorrow come to the surface.

Several of us pleaded, "Please join us. Let's together lay our burdens down at the feet of Jesus. Allow Him to place His healing balm on our hearts and ease the pain. Let's seek His face and hear from Him." After many attempts to compel members to the altar, some still held onto bitterness, even to the point of giving up hope on God!

We desired for this service to be a place to begin grieving, to eventually embrace God's love, comfort, warmth, and healing through His Holy Spirit. Instead, a rebellious spirit captured many, and many refused to be consoled. Thank God for those who participated in the service, willingly acknowledging their deep hurt. As the night went on, prayers of misery turned to rejoicing. God himself was glorified!

The devil keeps many bound up, wounded, angry, bitter, callous, and locked up in the prison of our pain! Frequently, Christians underestimate the power of our enemy. Unresolved grief is a way for Satan to get in and cause destruction. Ill-managed sorrow is like a type of cancer, invading the body, mind, and spirit. It can lead to physical sickness, and even death.

Prayer is a must.

Honestly communicating our heart before the Lord is the medicine and treatment for deep heartaches. Nothing and no one but the Holy Spirit can begin to apply the "antibiotic" or "radiation and chemo" needed. This is because unresolved grief attacks the very depths of one's faith.

Death and sickness are not the only things causing this kind of sadness. The list is long and includes life issues, such as incarceration, failed relationship, emotional or physical trauma, abuse or neglect, toxic work or living environment, and financial or business loss. No matter what kind of grief or level of despair occurs, it's necessary to lament, express, and release the inner turmoil. Some quietly express sadness, but it's OK to scream, weep, cry, moan, punch a pillow, or holler at the top of one's lungs! And we can't overlook the need to talk to a professional Christian counselor or join a support group. Often this is what may be needed. Remember, God is always present.

It's through this grief process that we experience the love, nurture, and freedom only God can give. God reveals more of himself and the grief He's endured to us. God helps us understand the ultimate gift of himself, of Jesus who died on the cross for us. We have the opportunity to become closer to God than ever before and to be set free in His throne room, where it's safe and secure! Not only set free from the recent sadness and sorrow experienced. If we would just come to the altar and accept God's invitation to abide in His tender, loving care and give all our heart-hurts to Him, not only will He heal current grief, but He will also heal past hurts, disappointments, and harm we've experienced. He will give us the rest and freedom we've been longing for. "And He walks with me, and He talks with me, and He tells me I am His own. And the joy we share as we tarry there, none other has ever known" ("I Come to the Garden Alone") can be our song. There's nothing like being set free from the bondage and traps that the devil sets up for us! This is the sunshine after the rain!

By processing our grief by expressing our honesty to God, our ultimate testimony is one of deliverance and healing: "Thou hast turned for me my mourning into dancing: thou hast put off my sackcloth, and girded me with gladness" (Psalm 30:11). Our heavenly Father's desire for His children is not for us to remain emotionally imprisoned but for us to be free.

— MARIA WESTBROOK

Reflect

Describe a time of grief in your life.

How did you respond?

What Scriptures did you apply?

Which new ones will you use if you have to deal with grief again?

God Hears Our Heart

When I was growing up, the adults around me taught me that God answers prayer in three ways: yes, no, and wait. If He said no, it was for a good reason. I confidently believed my heavenly Father desired to give me only good gifts. Several Scriptures in the Bible reinforced this truth in my mind:

> "Keep on asking, and you will receive what you ask for. Keep on seeking, and you will find. Keep on knocking, and the door will be opened to you. For everyone who asks, receives. Everyone who seeks, finds. And to everyone who knocks, the door will be opened. You parents—if your children ask for a loaf of bread, do you give them a stone instead? Or if they ask for a fish, do you give them a snake? Of course not! So if you sinful people know how to give good gifts to your children, how much more will your heavenly Father give good gifts to those who ask him." (MATTHEW 7:7–11 NLT)

At the age of three, I can remember wanting an older brother. I'm not sure why; nonetheless, I found myself asking my pregnant mom for one. Imagine my disappointment when she informed me, "You're the oldest, but you can ask God for a younger brother."

Well, to my surprise, a few months later I gained a baby sister. Four years later, my mom was pregnant again, and I was determined to make my request come to fruition. Every day for the duration of my mom's pregnancy, I prayed and asked God for a baby brother. I also included an additional request: *Lord, let him be born on Valentine's Day.* I absolutely believed God had heard me and planned to answer my prayer.

I remember my sister joining me in her prayers, but she prayed something different each time—for a boy, a girl, and even twins! But I never wavered. On Valentine's Day, I confidently told everyone at my school, "My baby brother is going to be born today." I even drew a picture of him in my art class. Sure enough, when I got home after school, my parents were at the hospital.

Later that night, my dad called and said, "Guess what?"

Proudly, I told him, "I already know I have a baby brother!"

Shocked, he asked, "What? How did you know?"

I replied, "Duh, I prayed and asked God for him." From then on, I believed this is how God would work: I make my request known to Him, and He answers by giving me what I want. This childlike faith I had about prayer is something I believed for years. However, it was challenged at age twelve. That was when my father lost his ministry job, which forced us to move out of our spacious home into an apartment, and my parents separated.

Overnight my "perfect" family fell apart. I prayed every day for years, "Please Lord, reconcile my parents and reunite our family." I waited and waited, hoping for God's yes answer.

When my parents divorced ten years later, my faith in God wavered, but I still held onto hope and prayed for a remarriage at some point. I thought that God wanted marriages to stay together and families to be restored.

When I turned thirty, I finally got the answer to my fervent, much-anticipated prayer. Yet, it was not the answer I expected. It was a resounding no, with the sudden death of my father. Two days after Christmas, my brother and sister found him dead on his couch in his apartment.

People tried to console me, "God has the master plan . . . He knows what He is doing . . . You just . . ." These words brought no solace to my soul. All kinds of emotions churned inside. I felt alone, disappointed, confused, angry, hurt, and sad. I thought, *God does not care about me. If He did, why would He let this happen? Why did my family and I have to experience so much pain? What was the point?* I saw nothing good or hopeful about God's "no!"

It's only human, in the face of unhappiness, to say to God, I don't understand. How else is a person supposed to think and feel when God responds, *No! I'm not fixing this the way you think it should be fixed.*

When my father died, I began to really struggle with my relationship with God. No conversations with Him, my anger boiled inside, and He got the silent treatment. I found it was hard to attend church and to be around other believers. People regularly inquired, "How are you doing?" They would tack on their favorite cliché, "I am blessed and highly favored in the Lord." I refused to answer in the same way. In my eyes, God had failed me. He was not the "good Father" everyone sang about. I no longer trusted Him or His plan for my life.

In Pemba, Mozambique, on a mission trip, I finally broke. Hot, steamy tears ran down my cheeks. I finally told God exactly how I really felt about Him. As others worshiped, I yelled, screamed, and cried. I shook my finger in God's face. My expression was ugly, messy, and I'm sure I included a few cuss words. But then, I felt God's presence as He held me and simply said, *I know, I know, I know . . .*

UNDERSTANDING LAMENTING

I did not know it at the time, but later I realized what happened in Mozambique was a *lament*. I poured all my grievances out to God, He heard my cry, and He gave me comfort. Understanding lamenting and taking the time to do so in my prayer time marked the beginning of a new spiritual journey for me, remarkably transforming. God taught me how to express my frustrations, regrets, anger (sometimes rage), grief, and sorrow. I am confident, more than ever before, it's OK to pour my heart out to Him like David in the book of Psalms. When we lament, our insides are groaning, and our emotions are raw. It's not a pleasant experience, but it's what God wants, and it results in greater intimacy with Him.

When I look at Scripture, I see I am not the only one God said no to. When David committed adultery with Bathsheba and conceived a child, God issued a warning through Nathan—*the child will die*. Nonetheless, David fasted and prayed for God to spare their son's life, only for the child to pass away seven days after birth (2 Samuel 12:15–25).

Paul prayed and asked for the thorn to be removed from his side, and God's response was no. He said, "My grace is sufficient" (2 Corinthians 12:7–9).

One might argue that God's no to David was punishment for his sin. Was Paul's thorn intended to keep Paul humble? Maybe. But what about God telling Jesus no? Jesus, the meekest man on earth, who was without sin. Yet, in the garden of Gethsemane, Jesus asked, "Is there any other way (other than death on the cross)?" God answered no, based on Jesus's response and the unfolding events of His death: "O my Father, if it be possible, let this cup pass from me: nevertheless not as I will, but as thou wilt" (Matthew 26:39).

He's always there. One of my spiritual mentors, Terry Wardle, uses the following illustration to explain better when God says no, and our response. Imagine your car breaks down on the side of the road. It's the middle of winter with freezing temperatures, and you are stranded. Then Jesus arrives with the tow truck. Jesus helps you into the cab of the truck where there is hot chocolate waiting for you and a warm blanket. He leaves the vehicle running with the heat blasting while He gets out and tends to your car. Sweet! Time for dancing and rejoicing!

Now let's imagine scenario number two. Jesus arrives, and He sees you stranded. He opens the door of the car. He does not come with a tow truck, hot chocolate, blanket, or heated cab. Instead, He gets inside the freezing car, wraps His arms around you, and holds you while you slowly die. This is not a time for rejoicing, but rather a time to lament and ask God why He did not provide a different way.

Take a fresh look. *Lament* is a musty old biblical word we really don't talk about in our churches. Yet, it's a biblical principle. On several occasions in the Scriptures, God lamented over the disobedience of His people and the bondage of the entire universe in the hands of the enemy (Zephaniah 3).

The book of Lamentations is filled with, you guessed it, laments! It is precisely what Jesus did in the garden before His death. The Scriptures tell us Jesus agonized to the point of shedding tears of blood. Guess what? At that moment, Jesus lamented. After His cry to God, the Savior had peace to move forward in God's plan.

Just recently I described lamenting to a friend. I explained that it's like vomiting, in that it is the worst feeling and experience ever! Lamenting is a letting go of a dream, a hope, or an *I just know that God is going to come through for me.* It's no easy task! Yet, it's still something I believe God wants His children to embrace.

We are often raised or encouraged to believe it's commendable not to show emotion. That that's a sign of being strong. "Did you see how she held up? She didn't even cry. She doesn't even seem like it's pulling her down." Yet, the Bible gives us permission to show emotions—to be hurt, to ask questions, and to be angry. This is not something easily understood. Giving oneself permission to lament, cry, scream, and express deep hurt and sorrow before the Lord is not something most of us have understood is OK. Instead, we've heard more about God being pleased when we put on a brave, stoic front. Pretending all is well when we know inside it really isn't.

I remember the old folks talking about a "breaking" after someone died. Once the person got back to the house from the hospital or the funeral home, or during or after the service, they allowed themselves to release strong emotions. Back in the day, people talked about it being healthy for the grieving wife, mother, sibling, or friend to totally break down and cry. The kind of cry that is ugly with snot and weeping out loud. When someone, a dream, a hope, or an expectation dies, God gives us permission to scream it out.

— LYDIA TURNER

Reflect

Think about your reservations to honestly express to the Lord your sadness, grief, or disappointments.

What in your upbringing, church experience, or anything else has contributed to your way of thinking?

In what ways do you need to change, and how are you planning to go about it?

God Encourages Our Lament

God "flips scripts." I was raised to think that if you didn't do drugs, swear, or have sex, your life would be OK. It's a transactional, bargaining-type relationship with God. *If I do X, God is obligated to do Y.* Last year God really blew apart this thinking. I was at a good point spiritually; talking with the Lord. And I had received some needed therapy, to heal from some past issues. My life seemed to be "coming together."

An excellent job opportunity opened in Boston, and with confidence I decided this was a perfect time to make a move. I flew to Boston—twice—to interview. And I got the job. I even landed a second job, because the cost of living out East is expensive. But . . . I couldn't secure housing. I called everybody, and tried every way I knew to figure it out. I just knew, *this is what God wants for me and even if He comes through with a place at the last minute, He will work this out for me.*

Well, I had found nothing by the Sunday before the Monday I was to report for work. So this was my email to the place I thought I was supposed to go: "I'm unable to accept your offer because I was unable to secure housing." I was so upset with God. I'd already resigned from my position in Milwaukee since I just knew God had me in Boston. I could not comprehend why it seemed like God was leading me in that direction and opening doors, but then on the last leg when I needed a place to live—nothing.

For two days I drove around screaming, yelling, cussing, and crying. At that moment, I went to God and just let Him have it. I did not (for the first time) let my feelings fester or engage in unhealthy ways of coping, such as stuffing my feelings with food or shutting people out. I didn't sit there and pretend "everything is fine," and I didn't try to figure out plan B either. I went right to the Lord and told Him exactly how I felt.

I was extremely aware He was there with me and that I was not alone. The fact that He sat there and cried with me was a great comfort. He didn't excuse it, judge me for how I was feeling, or tell me, "Who are you to feel this way?" When I doubted my lamenting, it seemed like the Lord was encouraging me not to stop, but to share more. Kind of like how a mother comforts her little one who slams his finger in the car door, letting her child cry about the pain and let it out. God saw my pain and knew I needed to let it out. It was only after I lamented that I was able to hear God's voice and He was able to show me what to do next to move forward.

I'm no longer afraid to lament. I know the tears will eventually stop, the pain won't last forever, and God is with me.

— J. WRIGHT

LEARNING TO LAMENT

I wonder if you have had a similar experience where it seems God is not answering your prayers, fulfilling your wishes, changing your circumstances, or solving your problems. Did His no turn your world upside down? Cause a crisis? Did it make you feel stumped, betrayed, abandoned, unheard, or unloved? Did you start to question God's existence, His care, and His concern for you? Did you ask yourself, *Why pray if God is going to do His own thing anyway?* In this, we must look at why God says no, and how to respond. The Twenty-third Psalm is a wonderful passage to walk through as we learn how to respond to God's no.

STAGE 1: RECOGNIZE GOD CARES

Often our prayers during this stage come from a place of awe (worship and thanksgiving) or out of a need for God. In Psalm 23 (NIV), this is illustrated through God being our Good Shepherd. As His sheep, when we are with Him, we "lack nothing." It is a time in our faith journey where He leads us to restful and peaceful places and renews our strength. He will make sure we get everything we need to "refresh our soul." In this stage, we are told, "Don't worry about anything; instead, pray about everything. Tell God what you need, and thank him for all he has done. Then you will experience God's peace, which exceeds anything we can understand. His peace will guard your hearts and minds as you live in Christ Jesus" (Philippians 4:6–7 NLT). This is how we see God's love through the answered prayer of peace and provision.

Many believers desire to stay in stage one, but just like a baby must grow, our faith must grow. Knowing this, God often leads us down to the darkest valley (Psalm 23:3–4). This is the hardest place in our faith journey, where our will, desires, hopes, and expectations meet God, and reality is different. For some, we are faced with the reality that we live in a broken world. For others, it's the realization that we are broken and sinful people and, in our brokenness, we hurt others and others hurt us. This can look like a death of a loved one, a divorce, or a tragic incident. Or it can be a significant disappointment in a friend, family member, church leader, or even disappointment in ourselves. As a result, we have questions for God, but when asked they seem to go unanswered. God's silence causes us to doubt and question our life and faith.

As much as we would like to think otherwise, nowhere in the Bible does God promise that we as believers will avoid the pain of living in a broken world. In fact, Scripture teaches exactly the opposite. In the Gospels God says, "These things I have spoken unto you, that in me ye might have peace. In the world ye shall have tribulation: but be of good cheer; I have overcome the world" (John 16:33).

Why? As believers we are co-heirs with Jesus. Which means that not only do we share in His glory, but we also get to share in His suffering. Yet, what we suffer now is nothing compared to the joy that will eventually come our way.

> The Spirit itself beareth witness with our spirit, that we are the children of God: And if children, then heirs; heirs of God, and joint-heirs with Christ; if so be that we suffer with him, that we may be also glorified together. For I reckon that the sufferings of this present time are not worthy to be compared with the glory which shall be revealed in us. (ROMANS 8:16–18)

Most assume that *later* means after the trial is over, but God promises that even in the darkest valley He will be there with us to protect and comfort. That He will prepare a feast for you in the presence of your enemies; He will anoint your head with oil; and your cup will overflow with blessings (Psalm 23:5–6).

We can be encouraged:

> *And not only so, but we glory in tribulations also: knowing that tribulation worketh patience; and patience, experience; and experience, hope: and hope maketh not ashamed; because the love of God is shed abroad in our hearts by the Holy Ghost which is given unto us.* (ROMANS 5:3–5)

It is important to remember that when God says no to something, He is saying yes to something else. However, before we can embrace all that God has for us in this valley, we first must lament! We must express to God our feelings of hurt, doubt, anger, and disappointment. In that dialogue, we give space for God to remind us of His truth and to give us peace, comfort, and direction. It is only after we have allowed ourselves time to do this that we can fully let go of our will, hopes, desires, dreams, and expectations. Then we can embrace the Lord's.

STAGE 2: IDENTIFY UNHEALTHY BEHAVIOR

These are actions that prevent the process of lamenting from happening.

- Numb the hurt and pain. There are a lot of ways people manage hurt and pain. For me, whenever I have a migraine, I am quick to pop a painkiller. Over the years, I have had to increase the amount of medication I take and the frequency with which I take it for it to work. The same thing happens when we are experiencing emotional pain. Often people will numb pain with sex, food, TV, porn, alcohol and other drugs. Even things that are "culturally acceptable or positive" can be considered a painkiller. Some examples include: indulging in social media or romance novels, being busy serving and connecting with others, religious activities, or excessive exercise. Anything that keeps you from feeling hurt and pain can be considered a painkiller. What are yours? Identify them and consider surrendering them to the Lord.

- Deny the negative thoughts and feelings of being told no. Have you ever told yourself or someone else when something didn't turn out the way you wanted, "It's fine, I'm fine, it's all going to be OK; no, really, I am not upset; it really doesn't matter anyway; it wasn't that important to me"? This can be a form of denial. Instead of acknowledging the hurt feelings, to oneself, God, and others, we may choose to pretend like life is still great even though the situation didn't turn out as we had hoped.

- Control the outcome. Instead of accepting no, sometimes people strategize ways to get God to say yes. People bargain with God, *If I do this* _____ *or if I give up* _____ *then will you say yes?* If it's still not the result we are looking for, we may seek out other people or things to meet our need: *If God is not going to love me this way, I am going to find someone who will.* As a result, people can become hyper-focused on material things (fame, popularity, success), get involved in unhealthy relationships, become overly concerned about performance, or turn into people-pleasers.

- Punish self or others. These are the times we say, "It's all my fault," when it may be due to the brokenness of our world. It doesn't help when some churches preach that difficult times are a "sign of sin in your life." Sometimes the difficulties we experience are not of our doing. On the flip-side, there are those who place blame completely on another person, saying, "It's all your fault. I wouldn't be here if it were not for you." This is a failure to examine one's own responsibility in the situation.

STAGE 3: ENGAGE IN HEALTHY LAMENTING

Identify and let go of unhealthy ways of coping. What ways do you or I numb, deny, control, or punish ourselves and others because of the pain? Once we identify the unhealthy ways we manage the pain, we can repent and ask God to forgive us for trying to manage without Him, and ask Him to help us adopt His ways of coping and dealing with the pain.

As we let go of unhealthy ways of coping, the pain will naturally rise to the surface. When it does, we don't ignore it or stuff it down. Instead, we allow ourselves to feel it and let it come up and out! Express it to God in words (spoken/written), images, and physical movements. For everyone this looks different: some yell, scream, and cry. Others will journal, draw, write stories and poetry, while some may express their anguish through dance, singing, and acting. Either way, we can let all that is inside come up and out, knowing that this might take time and multiple occasions of lament.

In just letting it all out, it doesn't matter who is there to listen and receive our woes, whereas with a *lament*, our woes are directed toward God alone. It is expressing our hurt, disappointment in, and anger to Him. Another difference is that there is a point in the lament where space is given *for God to respond*. God has something to say whether it be a reminder of the truth about who He is, who you are, or who the other person is. He will use that time to bring peace and comfort. This is what I like to call the "great exchange." We cast our burdens on Him and He replaces them with His "light yoke" (see Matthew 11:30). Once we can lament, we can forgive ourselves, others, God, accept God's will, surrender control, receive God's love, and say yes to His will.

— LYDIA TURNER

Reflect

Write out a lament to the Lord.

Pray it back to the Lord.

Share your lament with someone you can trust.

Blessed TO JOIN INTERCESSION

HIDDEN IN HIM

The dream was so vivid, I sat up in bed. I saw my son, Keevon, in his bed, engulfed in flames. I tried to go back to sleep, but I couldn't. I got up, and my husband, Thomas, asked, "Where are you going?" I said, "I'm just going to check on the boys."

When I got to Keevon's room, I saw that his blanket had covered the nightlight at the end of his bed, and it was already smoking.

Had I not gone in his room that night might he have been killed in a fire? In fact, the entire family might have perished that night.

I could tell you story after story like that, continuously seeing the hand of God's protection over our family. Mothers and caregivers don't know the dangers all around, but God does. Lord, may we be quiet before you and attentive to your voice.

> *For in the time of trouble he shall hide me in his pavilion: in the secret of his tabernacle shall he hide me; he shall set me up upon a rock.* (PSALM 27:5)

—SANDRA FOSTER

Delivered

After my divorce, I bounced too quickly into a rebound relationship with an ex-boyfriend. There are, no doubt, exceptionally good reasons why an ex-boyfriend is an ex-boyfriend. But time and extenuating circumstances play havoc on our common sense and make us forget those reasons. He had gotten wind of my troubles and reappeared in my life like the rescuing cavalry. I had been so enamored with this man in the past, that I blindly overlooked the past and many visible, current danger signs. It wasn't until several months into the relationship, and after I had wasted a considerable amount of emotional energy, that he slipped up and I discovered that he was married.

The decision to end the relationship right then and there should have been immediate, right? *Kick him to the curb*, you say. You're correct, but I'm telling you, it wasn't that easy.

I had probably been like you in my resolve never to get involved with a married man before the previous years of devastation happened to my psyche and wore my resistance down to a nub. *No way would I ever date a married man*, I had mused. *Women who do that have no marital integrity, low self-esteem, and just don't care about anyone but themselves,* I'd reason.

Married men know better than to even to look my way because I'm better than that, I'd try to convince myself. Even though I'd been duped, here I was a Christian author and conference speaker, educator, and mother of two young sons, terribly wrapped in a strong emotional tie with a married man. The lust of my heart immediately kicked into overdrive.

He showed up when I needed him, it whispered. *His marriage must not be fulfilling to him. He's telling you his marriage is over, and he's leaving. Just give him a little more time. Think about it—he dropped everything in his life to be here for you. The spark between you never went out over all these years. You don't deserve to be alone. He's here. He's filling the empty spaces.*

An invisible, magnetic attraction wouldn't let me out of this man's grip, and I didn't know what to do. Instead of dumping him, I decided to give up on myself and the ministry to women God had launched in me. In the words of the older people in the church, I was a "wretch undone." *There was no way God could use me now.* I figured I would become simply another one of the walking wounded, struggling through life the best I knew how, hoping to occasionally eat the crumbs of blessing from the gracious master's table.

However, a year earlier, I had signed a contract to be the keynote speaker at a prominent women's conference on the East Coast, and that event was drawing near. I don't believe in backing out of my commitments, so I asked God for His mercy. "Please, God," I begged, "anoint me this one last time. The women at this conference deserve your best. I realize this will be the last time you use me. I'm OK with that. Just, please, speak to those ladies through me."

Thank God for His Spirit living in my life. Even when I was at my weakest, His compassion reached out to me. The messages I communicated at that conference were some of the strongest and most precious I've ever delivered. I could literally feel God's presence and anointing. The night before my last message, another speaker gave a message and afterward invited women to the altar for prayer. She walked over to me, placed her hand on my shoulder, and then looked into my eyes and said, "Oh, no. God is not finished with you." Startled, I focused on her kind eyes, and the next thing she said broke me into thankful tears. "God loves you." She went on to tell me of many wonderful things God still had planned for my life and ministry.

On the strength of that renewed message of God's love and acceptance, and despite my failures and weaknesses, I returned home no longer depending on my own power to extricate myself from my situation. I asked God to do it for me. He silenced the lust of my heart with a longing for *His* heart. The more I focused on Him, the more my heart became like His. He led me one step at a time away from that unhealthy and ungodly relationship and back into fellowship with Him.

The shock of coming face-to-face with the depraved possibilities of my own heart brought me to my knees. That's precisely where God wanted me all along, and that's exactly where He wants each of us. Just as the health of our physical heart directly contributes to the maintenance of our healthy physical life, the health of our spiritual heart determines the vitality of our spiritual life. Just as we should protect our physical heart, God expects us to protect our spiritual heart too. After all, not only is it the heart that has the capacity for sympathy, feeling, and affection, but it's our heart that connects us to God.

The Bible has a lot to say about spiritual heart disease:

For out of the heart proceed evil thoughts, murders, adulteries, fornications, thefts, false witness, blasphemies. (MATTHEW 15:19)

A good man out of the good treasure of his heart bringeth forth that which is good; and an evil man out of the evil treasure of his heart bringeth forth that which is evil: for of the abundance of the heart his mouth speaketh. (LUKE 6:45)

He that trusteth in his own heart is a fool: but whoso walketh wisely, he shall be delivered. (PROVERBS 28:26)

Somebody may be thinking, *my goodness, I'm doomed. I may not have it all together, but by and large, I thought I was a woman with a pretty good heart.* Sorry, but Jeremiah smacks us right in the vanity and brings those high thoughts of ourselves right down to size. "The heart is deceitful above all things, and desperately wicked: who can know it" (Jeremiah 17:9). The Hebrew word for *deceitful* means "crooked and polluted." In other words, we're a mess apart from Christ. That's why Proverbs warns, "Keep thy heart with all diligence; for out of it are the issues of life" (Proverbs 4:23).

Isn't that amazing? We need to watch out for our own heart since the heart is the source of the mental, emotional, and spiritual appetites. And if we actively pursue our desires, we must find a way to be sure the heart is both protected from its own evil and focused on what's good and right. We not only have to be actively attentive, but we must be realistic about the deep-seated cravings within our hearts. What we don't pay attention to will hurt us.

James tells us "But every man is tempted, when he is drawn away of his own lust, and enticed" (James 1:14). Let's face it: most of our falls, foibles, and failures are our own fault. Nobody had to help us.

— SHARON NORRIS ELLIOTT

Reflect

Is there an area of weakness in your life?

Have you succumbed, and now find yourself involved in something ungodly and unhealthy?

Are you drawn to either start or continue a certain course of action clearly not in line with the Word of God?

Consider this prayer:

Dear God:

I'm involved with _____ *, or I'm thinking about doing* _____ *. I know you are displeased with* _____ *, but I don't know how to get untangled. Please help me. Replace the* *lust of my heart with the desires of your heart. Show me the practical steps I can take and then give me the fortitude to take them. I thank you in advance for deliverance. In Jesus's name, amen.*

Changed

Doug and I grew up together. He jokingly claims he proposed marriage to me when he was nine years old. We went through high school together. After graduation I got pregnant, and he entered into the service. It was 1961 when he returned, and we got married. We fought a lot. We both lived on the wild side, partying, and doing all kinds of things.

But then nineteen years after we were married, I got saved. When God filled me with His Spirit and His Word, I didn't want the lifestyle we were living. No more parties or going out to taverns. I became a Christian in January, and for the next six months, I went through hell with Doug. He wanted me back in those bars with him. He used to drive for miles up north and return and tell me he'd been with another woman, trying to make me jealous. A mother from the church prayed and encouraged me. "When he leaves the house, Mary, you get on your knees and stay there. Ask the Lord to keep him and bring him back." That's precisely what I did.

I used to help this mother in my church. I would buy food for her and her family. I'd also wash her clothes at my house and take them back to her. At the time, I didn't realize she had little or no money to do these things for her family. It turned out that I was a tremendous blessing to her physically while she helped me out spiritually. I needed to be around her. I look back now at how God worked that all out.

During that time, Doug would get so angry, that he would throw things and put holes in the walls. In June, six months after my commitment to Christ, he went to a graduation party and came home drunk. He ended up pushing me, and I fell backwards onto the bed. After that incident, he sat down and started crying like a baby. The next day, one of the mothers from the church came by and talked with him. She told him he needed the Lord, and he agreed to attend a church service that Friday night. But I knew, in the back of his mind, he was thinking, *I'm going to church, but I'm still going out to do my thing afterward.*

God had other plans. Doug committed his life to Christ that Friday night and never looked back. He was an alcoholic, and he would go through a couple of cases of beer a week. He also was popping pills, and smoking marijuana and cigarettes. But that Friday night, he came home and started emptying out all the alcohol in the house. God took the taste away. Shortly after that, he gave up everything else. He was a totally changed man.

That was thirty years ago. Doug is now a prayer warrior. He can identify with so many who are struggling. We've been involved in the couples ministry and seen countless marriages saved. He's the prayer coordinator for our church and participates in a nationwide prayer network. He's organized a prayer clock and has more than ninety people praying twenty-four hours a day. His phone is full of messages and prayer requests.

Doug continually says, "I'll be forever grateful to my wife; she refused to give up on me."

—MARY SMITH

Moses is hailed as one of the greatest leaders in history. God called him to deliver the Hebrews, God's chosen people, from bondage in Egypt back to the land He promised to their fore-fathers, in Canaan. In the book of Hebrews, Moses's parents, Amram and Jochebed, are commended for their faith They are acknowledged for hiding Moses for three months after his birth, despite the Pharaoh's edict to throw all the Hebrew male babies into the Nile River. These parents refused to fear the Egyptian ruler when they saw that God had given them an unusual child (Exodus 2:1–10; Hebrews 11:23).

The scholars who've studied the phrase, "God had given them an unusual child" (Hebrews 11:23 NLT), share a variety of explanations. Was he larger, stronger, and healthier than their other two children and others in the community? It's a mystery. But the one thing we do know is when they looked at baby Moses, something spoke to them from within—they said *we cannot kill him or allow him to be killed.*

Pharaoh, because of his fear of the growth and strength of the Hebrew nation, declared the death edict. At first, he ordered the midwives to kill all the male Hebrew children at birth. God intervened, making sure the midwives feared the heavenly Father more than Pharaoh. As a result, they refused to carry out his evil scheme. Pharaoh persisted, and he ordered all the male babies to be thrown into the Nile River and drowned.

Moses's parents kept him out of sight for three months until it was impossible to muffle his cries. I'm a mother, and I can almost hear Jochebed desperately pleading with Jehovah for the life of her son, as she pushed him in a basket out into the Nile. She assigned her daughter Miriam to watch over her little brother. I have no doubt that she prayed that the women in Pharaoh's court who were bathing nearby would rescue him and have mercy. That's precisely what happened. Pharaoh's daughter saw him, and Miriam stepped right in, offering to get a Hebrew woman to nurse him. Of course, she called her mother. God allowed Jochebed to nurse her baby for the next several years.

As I observe the African American males, like Doug, in my family and community I see something in them that keeps me praying. Like Mary, Doug's wife, and like Moses's parents, I ask God for the strength of mind and heart to continue to pray. It helps to know Jesus is also interceding with me.

I see African American Christian men as God's change agents. At times, I climb up on my soapbox and go to fussing. I get impatient. I want action! However, God reminds me that one of the phrases in Hebrews 11 is often skipped over when discussing the heroes of the faith. "These all died in faith, not having received the promises, but having seen them afar off, and were persuaded of them, and embraced them, and confessed that they were strangers and pilgrims on the earth" (Hebrews 11:13). *Excuse me, God, no one on this list witnessed the fulfillment of what you promised? Yet, they all died still believing that you were going to work out the details someday. Mmm.*

The Hollywood movie version of Moses's life fills in a lot more details about Amram and Jochebed. But scripturally there is no indication that these believing parents, who saw something in their infant son, ever personally witnessed Moses's rise to greatness. They hoped, prayed, and obeyed. That was it.

All too often I find myself weary, and tired of praying because I do not see *anything*. God must continuously remind me of the definition of *faith*. "Now faith is the substance of things hoped for, the evidence of things not seen" (Hebrews 11:1). God's timing means He is fully aware of what's going on. He knows what He's doing, and when to do it. He's sovereign over all — and in complete control. He will bring things to pass. Prayers put us in harmony with Him, His plans, and His purposes.

As mothers, grandmothers, sisters, wives, and others who are praying for our African American men, we may not see the fruit of our labor before we go to glory. But that reality should not discourage us from praying and continuing to believe God's promises.

Encourage. Miriam's story helps me in this regard. Early on, Moses's older sister was instrumental in watching over her baby brother as he floated in a basket on the Nile River. She quickly offered to go find him a nurse when Pharaoh's daughter discovered the baby (Exodus 2:5–10). Together, Moses, Miriam, and Moses's older brother, Aaron, all banded together to lead the people of Israel from slavery in Egypt to the Promised Land in Canaan. After the miraculous crossing of the Red Sea, it's Miriam who leads the women in singing, dancing, and worshiping God (Exodus 15:20–22).

The Scriptures call her a "prophetess," one who proclaims God's Word and speaks for Him.

Sadly, Miriam's flesh took over at some point on the journey. She and Aaron criticized Moses for marrying a Cushite woman. This was not her only objection, as she was at odds with God, and questioned the Lord's wisdom in choosing her little brother as their leader (Numbers 12:2). God displayed His displeasure with Miriam and struck her with leprosy. The very brother she put down became the one to plead with God for her healing. God answered Moses's prayer. After a week outside the camp, He healed her (Numbers 12:13). When I get into my grumbling, complaining, jealousy, judging, "God-you-are-taking-too-long" moods, Miriam's story is a reminder. I repent, asking God to help *me*.

Watching my words. I talk to Mary often about what happened to Doug, and about my personal challenges in praying. There is one thing she always reminds me of, "Watch your mouth, your attitude, and your tone of voice. Ask the Holy Spirit what to say and how to say it. Let Him do the convicting and the changing." *OK, Mary. I hear you.* At the same time, I must honestly admit that it's so easy for me to reach for that carnal weapon called my mouth. Out of it comes manipulation, deceit, or making the person feel guilt and shame.

When praying for our men, it goes without saying that we are in a spiritual battle. Satan would love for them to stay chained, bound up. The enemy is OK with them attending church, but not with them dropping to their knees, and bowing before the heavenly Father in adoration and earnestness.

The fight is not against the men standing in front of us, but the invisible, satanic powers lurking around. When we put our hand on our hip and give brother-man a piece of our mind, can you guess whose team is watching and waiting? Dressed up in our best fleshly uniform, we can mistakenly connect and link arms with the enemy line, leaving us powerless against the "wiles of the devil" (Ephesians 6:11).

The Scripture is in plain sight in my office, and I see it every day. Yet, walking this out on a regular basis is quite another story. This is the continuous prayer for me:

> For though we walk in the flesh, we do not war according to the flesh. For the weapons of our warfare are not carnal but mighty in God for pulling down strongholds, casting down arguments and every high thing that exalts itself against the knowledge of God, bringing every thought into captivity to the obedience of Christ, and being ready to punish all disobedience when your obedience is fulfilled. (2 CORINTHIANS 10:3–6 NKJV)

Paul admitted his flesh-versus-spirit battle. He identified with his fellow Christian brothers and sisters. However, his words remind believers that we are already suited up and equipped for spiritual warfare. God placed powerful weapons within our reach—the belt of truth, breastplate of righteousness, shoes of the gospel, shield of faith, helmet of salvation, and the sword of the Spirit. Jesus exemplified this kind of spiritual battle throughout His life on earth. He died to himself, remained humble, was entirely obedient to the Father, and dependent on the Holy Spirit, which resulted in victory.

Strongholds are wrong thoughts and perceptions about God, us, and others. They're also ungodly philosophies, sophisticated arguments, and pride-filled opinions. Yes, men need deliverance in these areas. On the other hand, the first stronghold God might have to break down is one inside of us, the praying woman. Time in the throne room might need to be spent with God working on our wrong thinking about what God can do, what He's already doing, and trusting His outcome. The Lord may need to strip our minds and hearts of our own plans and perceptions and change our insistence on what we think should happen and when. Remember, the power of God resides in us, and we are not helpless against our negative thoughts. Our way of thinking can be brought into the obedience of Christ as we wholly yield ourselves to Him.

— VICTORIA

Reflect

What are the spiritual battles you are facing today?

Have you submitted them to the divine Prayer Team?

Rescued

"What's wrong, Renee?"

I had been in church all my life, but attending worship service had become a struggle. I tried to tell my mother. I wanted God to fix everything. She knew something was not right with me, but I was afraid of what she might do if I told her. Or what he might do to her if I told. A grown man, who was supposed to be family, a pastor, had raped me at the tender age of nine—and I was never the same.

For the next several years, anger welled inside me, and I would simply sit and cry. I finally told my mother, and sure enough, she went after the rapist with a gun. Her outrage magnified because she, too, had been raped as a child by her dad's "best friend." Thankfully, my mother did not shoot the offender who had violated me, though his evildoing deeply wounded me, turning my life upside down. Then my father died, and shortly after his death, we moved from Milwaukee in the Midwest to the South. And my mother remarried.

Though my mother kept us in church, I started sneaking around, smoking and drinking at around eleven years old. By seventeen, I married—an older guy. I was drinking and dealing in drugs, and then suffering from cancer. At one point, I weighed more than 500 pounds, then lost several hundred pounds through weight-loss surgery. During all of this, I attended church every Sunday, singing in the choir, and leading solos. All while I was leading a double life, God was looking out for me.

On my mother's birthday in 2010, she dedicated her day to me, to revisit the man who had raped me. She knew that event had triggered my downturn and involvement with drug use, and that the offender had abused other women and young girls in the church. Now he had cancer and was dying, and when my mother confronted him, he confessed. After he admitted his wrong to my mother, she put him on the phone with me. He acknowledged what he had done, and asked my forgiveness.

I still wanted to strangle or shoot him—but then my mother got back on the phone. She started praying over him! As she interceded for this man, I immediately felt God lifting this huge burden I'd been carrying. I experienced relief because my mother heard and understood my pain, and she modeled praying for our enemies (Luke 6:28). I started crying, and my thoughts began to change to: *When someone hurts you intensely, you must pray for them instead of seeking revenge.* I was on my road to recovery after that phone call. I didn't suddenly forget about the rape and the pain this man caused. The memory and hurt from that is lifelong, even if you can work toward forgiveness.

My mother got me into a program that gave me the tools to stop using drugs, and once clean, I never went back to drugs. After treatment, I wanted to reach back and help those struggling with addictions. I eventually opened fourteen recovery houses and had a transportation business as well. I tried to help everyone stay clean. But I was doing it on my own and it proved to be too much for me.

One night I got every pill in the house and was getting ready to end my life. It was 3:00 a.m. Then the phone rang. Again, it was God working through my mother for my rescue. She said, "The Lord woke me up. Whatever you are about to do, don't do it." This was a major turning point in my life. I began to say to the Lord, "I want this kind of relationship with you; like you and my mother have." I began to realize that when I prayed, I did all the talking. Now I desired for God to talk to me.

One day, I was unloading a truck, and I had bags in my hand. God spoke to my heart, *Renee, be still and listen.* He got my attention! I was so excited and touched by all of this I started walking down the street, crying. People probably thought I was crazy. A woman drove up in a car and asked, "You OK?" From that day on, my relationship with God became entirely different. I'd put the kids to bed, grab my Bible, and go to my room to spend time with Him. No TV, radio, or any other source of entertainment. I just wanted Him, and to hear His voice.

My son died two years ago, at thirty-six years of age. He injured himself playing football and started taking prescription pain medication, which led to an addiction. He had moved to California and had a child. But he got too sick, and I had him come back to Milwaukee. Weeks before his death, the Lord spoke to me, *Renee, prepare yourself because Johnny needs to come home.* The Sunday before he died, my pastor commented, "Johnny got this bright look on his face; a glow." That week Johnny started giving his stuff away, laughing, and telling people, "I don't need it." Family members didn't understand, but I knew what was happening.

When we found him dead later in the week, people filled my house for days. Folks were shocked at how calm I stayed, but it was because God had prepared me. My pastor looked at me during all of this and asked me, "Renee, you're at peace, aren't you?" I really was. God had already spoken to me and was giving me comfort.

Someone told me, "Never question God." My mother said, "No, that's not right." God wants you to ask questions and to say what's on your heart and mind. He desires to answer back. He may not tell you what you want to hear, but He does want to talk to you.

Raped at age nine and married at seventeen. I buried my father, mother, stepfather, husband, fiancé, and my son. God has carried me through all of that. I always attended church and sang, but now it's different. I wait to hear what God has to say first, and that's what I say or sing.

Just recently, a friend asked me to come and minister to a mother who had just lost her child in a random shooting—a thirteen-year-old just sitting in her house, now dead. By keeping it real, and testifying to others about what God has done for me through difficult times, the Lord helps me to comfort others in these kinds of situations. I listen and tell others what He's saying to me, do what He tells me, and endeavor to remain surrendered to Him.

My theme is, "The LORD is my Shepherd" (Psalm 23.1). I can see Him guiding me throughout my life.

— RENEE WILLIAMS LOGBO

Reflect

Allow yourself to think about the hurt someone has caused you. Reflect, and ask God to help you heal.

Have you lifted up your pain to God in prayer?

What are your testimonies about God inviting you to pray for yourself, your children, and others?

Restored

Things in our lives do not always go as anticipated. As a child, I had many aspirations. I imagined myself as a wife, mother, and owning a house with a white picket fence; the dream. However, I don't ever remember saying, "I want to be a single parent." I learned that in this life's continuous journey, everything may not fall in order according to one's plans. No one gets married thinking, *I'll eventually get a divorce, become a widow, or I'll be subjected to abuse.*

Where do we turn when our world crumbles and darkness is all around? These are the questions I began to ask when I found myself pregnant with my son. In my eighth month, my child's father dropped a bomb: "Don't contact me any longer. I've moved on, and I'm in another relationship." Single parenting was not what I'd dreamed about as a child. I had no idea I was signing up for one of the hardest jobs in the world. I wished I had a manuscript to show me exactly what to do.

While my son was still in the womb, I prayed for him. No guidebook dropped from the sky. I began to pray and seek the Lord. When my child was still in my belly, I asked God, *What should I name the baby? Emmanuel* is the name that came to mind. Later, my mother confirmed it. Without the two of us discussing it at all she said, "God keeps telling me his name is Emmanuel." *Emmanuel* means, "God is with us" (Matthew 1:23). This became a constant reminder to me that I'm never alone. God is always going to be with us.

As a single parent, it's easy for things to feel overwhelming. I try to be continuously grateful because I see my son every day. I have the privilege of watching him grow, and I witness many priceless moments in his life. Are there difficult moments? Yes! But I ask God to fill my heart with thanksgiving, and not to allow me to lose hope.

God turns our nothings into something. Recall the story about the widow in Elisha's time. She had two sons, and her husband died. They were about to be taken into slavery because of her debt, but the prophet Elisha intervened. He miraculously provided enough oil for her to pay her creditors and provide for her needs (2 Kings 4:1–7). This is one of many biblical accounts of the heavenly Father attending to those who are without.

God fills the voids. As a single parent, we often observe the blank spaces of our children's lives. The number-one empty place is, of course, the other parent. When Emmanuel attended kindergarten, this became one of the hardest times for both of us. He immediately observed the other children with their fathers, and he looked up at me and asked, "Where is my dad?" He cried almost every day those first few weeks of school. He felt different, out of place. He just wanted to be like everyone else. It hurt me to see my son suffer. He just wanted his dad to be present in his life. He longed for his father to love him and share in these special moments in his life.

This also made me face a hard reality; my love wasn't enough. I began to pray, "Lord, my child needs the love of his father. He's not here. Please, Lord, you fill this void in his life. I can't." I stood on the promise in Isaiah, "I will teach all your

children, and they will enjoy great peace" (Isaiah 54:13 NLT).
I believed God would somehow comfort Emmanuel.

There's so much that can be said about praying for our children as single parents. I've learned so much. Here are a few prayers we need to pray on their behalf:

- *Pray for our own healing.* It's easy to hold onto anger, resentment, and self-pity because of the absence of the other parent, along with their refusal to do their part. Our children need a whole parent, not pieces of one; pieces are sharp and can cut. This can result in yelling and demonstrating a lousy attitude toward the child. My mother helped me with this when she said to me one day, "God told me no one owes me anything." This is a hard lesson, but it causes me to look to Christ for my needs.

- *Pray to be a godly example.* I'm a new creation in Him (2 Corinthians 5:17); He now fights my battles (Exodus 14:14). Secure peace by surrendering everything to the Lord. Resolve to live godly in Christ Jesus and set a good example before your child. If the other parent is doing crazy things, we don't have to ride "the crazy train" along with them. Show your child, when things get rough, that we need to pray, relax, and calm down. "Give all your worries and cares to God, for he cares about you" (1 Peter 5:7 NLT). Ask God to fill not only your child's empty places but to fill your voids as well. What does your child see you do when you are lonely, bored, feeling unloved, or depressed? No one can be a perfect person or parent, but we can demonstrate, primarily through prayer, our need for the Lord's help and intervention.

- *Pray for their protection.* As African American parents, we need to have "the talk" with our children so they can make it home safely. At times it feels as if our Black children carry a target on their backs. No mother wants to join the unwanted club of losing her child to violence or the prison system. We must put our war clothes on, asking God to keep, protect, guide, and cover our children with His love, peace, and protection. The enemy is out "to steal, and to kill, and to destroy" (John 10:10).

- *Pray to be able to see your child as God does.* Emmanuel is a gift from God, and he is not a mistake. He is God's precious possession. He is to be raised according to biblical principles. I pray Emmanuel will come to know Christ at an early age, listening to and obeying God's voice. On this single-parenting journey, I'm expecting God to "show up and show out"!

— KIMBERLY TOWNSEND

PRIVILEGED

The arrival of a baby is a wondrous experience! Holding my firstborn, I remember marveling at the mystery of birth and life. Gently stroking smooth black hair, caressing soft, wrinkled skin, and examining tiny, perfectly formed fingers and toes, I was mesmerized. With the intense labor and childbirth behind, waves of joy rushed in like a flood. With a thankful heart, I gazed lovingly at my precious little one. Admittedly, he was a gift from God!

Hopes and dreams captured my imagination, and I was lost in a world of wonder. "Lord, thank you for this precious child, a little masterpiece of your design. Now, Lord, I pray, prepare me for the days ahead as I care for this child you've entrusted to me."

Raising children is an enormous responsibility. Praying for them is a daily privilege. With all the ups and downs of the journey, every day is a good day for us parents to pray for our children. Whether we're rejoicing on the good days to celebrate a child's first step, first word, first day of school, birthday, or graduation, or whether we are overwhelmed on the hard days when work seems unending and sleep is short, prayer ushers us into God's presence where we can find wisdom, strength, healing, power, blessing, and peace.

My mom believed in the power of prayer. Growing up, I observed her pray for my siblings and me every day and throughout the day. Her prayers became guardrails surrounding our lives. After all, we were her "riches," her heritage from the Lord, as the psalmist declares (Psalm 127:3).

She stayed on her knees, petitioning God to keep us safe from harmful disease, bad influences, dangerous situations, and bad choices. As much as she loved us, she knew God loved us more! She covered us with prayers because only God could watch over us when we were out of her sight. I believe God heard her prayers. She has gone home to be with the Lord now, but her faithful example remains my inspiration to carry the torch and pray daily for my children and generations to come.

Praying for our children is eternally consequential since our children have souls hungry for God. By praying for them (and with them), we introduce them to our heavenly Father and spiritual truth. Scripture assures us that from the womb, God is watching over them; they are His special creation. "You made all the delicate, inner parts of my body and knit me together in my mother's womb" (Psalms 139:13 NLT). He loves them with "an everlasting love" (Jeremiah 31:3).

Knowing that God is for our children should encourage us to pray for everything that concerns them—their relationship with God, their protection, health, faith, their friends, and their future. Our prayers for our children make a difference and will change their lives.

We present petitions to our God, who longs to be gracious and compassionate to us (Isaiah 30:18). "For the eyes of the Lord are over the righteous, and his ears are open unto their prayers: but the face of the Lord is against them that do evil" (1 Peter 3:12). With confidence we can pray the following for our children:

- That they draw close to God, for He longs for them to be in a relationship with Him.
- That, like young Samuel, they will listen for the voice of God when He speaks. His still, small voice will speak the truth, steer them from temptation, and remind them of wrongdoings (1 Peter 5:8). "The LORD keeps you from all harm and watches over your life. The LORD keeps watch over you as you come and go, both now and forever" (Psalm 121:7–8 NLT).

- That they will choose their friends wisely and associate with people of good character for, "Be not deceived: evil communications corrupt good manners" (1 Corinthians 15:33).
- That God will establish the works of their hands and do mighty things in their lives.
- That God will guide them in all their relationships, and especially in their choice of a life partner.
- That the favor of the Lord rests on them (Numbers 6:24–26). And as a result, they bless and worship the Lord.

Whatever else we choose to add, we know prayer activates the power of God on our behalf. If we want the best for our children, partnering with God in prayer is the most important thing we can do!

— JULIETTE ALLEN

Reflect

What Scriptures has God used to help you understand yourself as a parent, or to help you to understand those parents you observe?

Are you able to identify with a single parent?

What more could you do or pray, to help a parent who is raising a child alone, or in a blended family context?

In what areas might you make some changes in your life, or the life of your family?

Called to Pray

I remember a man that I once knew. I remember him calling me every month from his college and talking for two to three hours at a time late into the night. He impressed me as a man serious about God's business, and he seemed willing to go deep into God's Word and to find those nuggets that would move him closer to God's heart and God's intentions.

That man was Terry David Reeder. He impressed me so much that I married him. After we married, we moved into a small one-bedroom apartment in Detroit. It was an old building, probably built in the 1920s, but it had a large, walk-in closet in the living room, which was odd for a structure of that vintage. "I want this closet," he said as we walked around and talked about how we planned to arrange things. I'm not sure how I felt about that; after all, a walk-in closet is a woman's dream! But he had acquiesced to me in so many ways leading up to our marriage that I agreed. He would take the walk-in closet.

It was only later that I understood why.

One morning I woke up and Terry was not next to me. I couldn't imagine where he was, so I walked into the living room. "Terry?" He was in the walk-in closet, and he was praying. "But thou, when thou prayest, enter into thy closet, and when thou hast shut thy door, pray to thy Father which is in secret; and thy Father which seeth in secret shall reward thee openly" (Matthew 6:6).

I would find that my husband took this verse in Matthew very, very seriously. That walk-in closet was his "room," the place where he would pour his heart out to God. There were times when that room would be closed for a half to a whole hour at a time. I knew at those times not to knock, and to treat that closet with the reverence with which I knew he was entering that place of intimacy that I, even as his wife, could not share. Many mornings, I found Terry in that secret place before the sunrise.

That was not the only time he would pray. One day, Terry came to me and said, "Diane, I want to spend a day to myself. I just want to think and pray and be alone." I was kind of hurt but agreed reluctantly to his request.

When he came back home, he came home with the most beautiful love letter I have ever received! It wasn't sugary because Terry was not the "sugary" type, but it was written from his full and loving heart. After that, I welcomed those separate times and was moved to use those days for my own sessions with the Lord. They were precious times and made coming back together at the end of the day that much sweeter.

Later, at our church in Detroit, Terry approached our pastor. He had heard about a practice called "prayer cells" that were designated times where the congregation would meet in small groups and pray together for one another and for the needs of the church. Pastor White was open to members who listened to the Lord and had ideas that would add to the life of the church, so he agreed to allow the groups.

We had two children by then. Alexandra was two and David was six. David followed his father everywhere—or maybe better, Terry took him everywhere. As a result, when we began the prayer cells, Terry gave David a job. His assignment was to stand and help direct people into rows as we broke into our small groups. I remember that David took that job very seriously, and would ask Terry on more than one occasion, "Daddy, are we going to do prayer cells?" Terry talked to his mother, another praying woman, about his work. "Mom," he would say, "I just want to stand in the gap." Terry had seen a "gap" in the wall at Mt. Lebanon-Strathmoor Church, and that gap had to do with the absence of concerted, intentional, group prayer.

I do believe that the enemy attacked the practice of prayer cells by attacking Terry. You see, a few short months later, we would find that others would have to stand in the gap for our family. Shortly after he began the prayer cells and got them up and running, Terry was diagnosed with leukemia. His was an acute form of leukemia that without treatment would typically take a person's life within six months. He went from a big man with a booming voice that matched his heart, to a man who for a time could neither walk nor talk. For four years, our entire family, including our church family and friends, struggled with this demon of an illness.

And so, we found that the Lord trained those very prayer cells that Terry started out of a passionate heart for God's people back onto him and our family. We surely needed the comfort of God's presence. I cannot tell you how many times the Lord would show himself strong during those precious and last four years that Terry, myself, and our children would have together. God let us know that, despite the challenge, hardships, and pain of this time, He was "an ever-present help in trouble" (Psalm 46:1 NIV). God spoke, and Terry listened. I know that Terry's closet prayers were heard and answered. And we were blessed. I can stand now as a woman who is grateful for a husband who prayed.

— DIANE PROCTOR REEDER

A woman who knows she is anointed to be the wife of her spouse intercedes. The power of intercession turns the king's heart in my home, protects, and promotes him. The heart of an intercessor is relentlessly merciful and prays in good times and in bad. Prayer is a two-way process that blesses the one praying and those covered in prayer. I've experienced this over more than thirty-five years of marriage to my husband.

Intercession is actually a form of warfare in the spirit for our family, community, and nation. It is clear that God promised that if we answer the call to humble ourselves and pray that we will experience healing (2 Chronicles 7:14). As Christians we have a responsibility to intercede.

The power of intercession by women for their husbands has proven to be life-changing for centuries. One of my favorite Bible stories is about Abigail, a woman who stood in the gap for her husband and his hired hands, as she no doubt swiftly prayed, discerning the devastation that could have occurred to her hot-headed husband, Nabal, by David's army (1 Samuel 25:1–35).

Look at what the Bible says about how we as Christians should battle:

UNTIL CHANGE COMES

> *For though we live in the world, we do not wage war*
> *as the world does. The weapons we fight with are*
> *not the weapons of the world. On the contrary,*
> *they have divine power to demolish strongholds. We*
> *demolish arguments and every pretension that sets*
> *itself up against the knowledge of God, and we take*
> *captive every thought to make it obedient to Christ.*
> (2 CORINTHIANS 10:3–5 NIV)

Apparently, the hired hands knew Abigail was a woman of prayer and wisdom as they went straight to her when they heard David was coming to destroy them (1 Samuel 25:12–15). No doubt, from many experiences with her man, Abigail gleaned wisdom to strategize a plan to save her husband and family as we see her preparing a meal and demonstrating good public relations skills as she presents herself in humility to David (1 Samuel 25:23–35). This action of negotiation was rewarded later as Abigail became one of King David's wives.

Like Christ, who makes intercession for us carrying the burden for others (Galatians 6:2), Abigail recognized her responsibility and made intercession for her husband, causing many lives to be saved. Likewise, in prayer, sisters can stand in the gap and pray until change comes.

— KARYNTHIA PHILLIPS

Reflect

God calls people to intercede; how has God called you to do so?

How can you start or enhance a prayer ministry in your area?

Anna

I remember it as if it were yesterday; a Wednesday morning in 2011, an 11:00 a.m. prayer meeting specifically. In the teaching time that day, I shared how Peter taught God's Word to the early church, going from house to house, and about the signs, wonders, and miracles that began to happen. Even though I'd taught this passage before, I felt great excitement on this particular day as the Holy Spirit's power rolled around in my thoughts.

On my ride home, I distinctly heard the Lord speaking to my spirit: *Anna.* I asked aloud, "What does *Anna* have to do with signs and wonders?" When I got home, I researched Luke 2:36–38, and the prophetess who remained in the temple, fasting and praying throughout the day, and into the night. The Bible described Anna as "a great age," meaning, a much older woman (v. 36). She lived with her husband for seven years; then, he died.

I can identify with her as an older woman. I've been married forty-five years. For forty-one of those, my husband and I served in ministry, pastoring a church until he passed. After his death, I wondered, *Lord, what do you want me to do now?*

The Holy Spirit spoke to me about becoming an Anna. At first, I was confused. *Lord, do I have to stay in the church day and night?* I wondered, but continuing to study, God enlightened me.

The Holy Spirit lives inside each Christian believer; we are now

God's "temple" (1 Corinthians 3:16). Wherever we are, we can spend time in His presence and in His Word. I'd prayed with people at church, in person, and over the phone. But after God called me an "Anna," He significantly increased my telephone prayer ministry.

Blessed! I wake up early singing, worshiping, and adoring Him. I read Scriptures and engage in listening to and talking with God. I have a prayer-partner time every day of the week starting Monday at 5:30 a.m. By 8:00 a.m., three of us are praying by phone, and an hour later, another prayer partner joins us there. I read Scripture and pray throughout the day with those who are shut-in. My day ends after my women's Bible-study class, which God has going strong after twenty years. Wednesday evenings, I pray with a group of women on a group-meeting call. We pray each week of the entire year for a women's conference that takes place each fall, along with other concerns.

I love praying and teaching the Word, and I am still a Sunday school teacher in an adult women's class, as God has given me a special ministry with women. This calling to outreach also began when the Lord spoke to my spirit: *you're an aging woman, called to teach younger women.* Though I didn't do anything until years after God spoke, I was in the basement one day when He spoke again: *You are an aged woman. You are to teach the younger women.* It was so loud and intense that I was afraid and ran up the stairs. After that encounter, I immediately responded, "Yes, Lord." Then I said, "You have to give me the women to teach."

I studied the passage in Titus:

> *The aged women likewise, that they be in behavior as becometh holiness, not false accusers, not given to much wine, teachers of good things; that they may teach the young women to be sober, to love their husbands, to love their children, to be discreet, chaste, keepers at home, good, obedient to their own husbands, that the word of God be not blasphemed.* (TITUS 2:3–5)

The women began to turn in my direction. One of my daughter's friends asked if I would be her mentor, and she has now attended my Bible class for years. One woman uses her lunch break to study the Word and pray with me. Others joined my Bible class at church; it's reached a total of thirty women.

The Lord is faithful. He will fulfill what He asks us to do. At the age of 86, I am still learning, and He is still teaching me. It's a blessing to answer when He calls.

—MOTHER CLOTEA WARE

Reflect

God calls people with different gifts to different responsibilities within the body of Christ; what are your gifts?

If you want to know your spiritual gifts, what knowledgeable persons will you approach to help you discern your gifts?

Sent

As I knelt before the Lord and prayed, "Father, I want to live your plan for my life," I never imagined that I would become a foreign missionary with a heart for world prayer. Living God's plan for my life meant learning to listen to the Holy Spirit's guidance. As the Holy Spirit guided me daily, I experienced the consequences of not obeying the Holy Spirit's voice and the blessings of obedience.

In college, the Holy Spirit led me to attend a workshop regarding foreign missions at a Christian conference. But I had no plans to go to the foreign mission field. I planned to marry my high school sweetheart and serve God as a teacher in urban America. At the end of the workshop, pictures flashed before us of children throughout the world. The call was for teachers to go and teach the children while sharing the gospel through our words and lives. As the last picture appeared, I heard the word *go!*

Me? Become a missionary in Africa? No way. After a lot of prayer and using the strategy of listing the pros and cons of the decision, I accepted God's plan. Two years later, I arrived in Nigeria, West Africa, to teach math and Bible. During my two years of preparation, God slowly developed in my heart the desire and discipline for intercessory prayer for the world.

My heart of prayer for the world resulted primarily from traveling to another part of the world and experiencing that God is omnipresent, omnipotent, and personal. Seeing God transform Nigerian lives made me realize that God is every-where, and that Jesus died for the whole world. A burden developed within me to consistently pray for the salvation and spiritual growth of others across the globe.

You don't have to travel to another part of the world to develop a heart of prayer for the world, but it does require one to have a proper perspective of worship, God, and the world. Our prayer life is greatly determined by what we believe about God. It is impossible to think that our prayers can affect the world without understanding who God is. Yet, to even have the desire to pray for the world results from knowing the importance of how the world affects our daily lives and the fulfillment of the Great Commission.

> *Go ye therefore, and teach all nations, baptizing them in the name of the Father, and of the Son, and of the Holy Ghost: Teaching them to observe all things whatsoever I have commanded you: and, lo, I am with you always, even unto the end of the world. Amen.* (MATTHEW 28:19–20)

Naturally, we won't take time to pray for what doesn't affect our lives personally. Though, as Christians, we are called to go out and make disciples of all the world. Prayer provides an opportunity for us to reach the world without physically traveling across the globe. Since God is omnipresent, we can pray to Him for someone a thousand miles away from us and know that God hears and joins in our prayers, and will act according to His will. There are countless stories of people praying for another person's safety in another part of the world, and later learning that at the precise moment of their prayer, God had intervened for that person.

What if you don't know anyone in another part of the world? Thank God for the advancement of the internet and social media. When I first started praying for the world, I used the *Operation World* book, a resource reporting about all the missionaries who've gone out and the places the gospel has gone around the world and the areas still in need. Today, with the internet, one can view pictures and obtain details to pray effectively for others in other parts of the world. Praying for others that we don't know may seem abstract at first and a waste of time. But we must remember who God is and that choosing to pray for the world reflects one's obedience to God's commands on reaching the world for Christ.

The apostle Paul exemplified obedience in being a world prayer warrior without necessarily traveling the whole world. He was ever mindful of the need to intercede for both Christians and non-Christians. Paul repeatedly prayed for those he knew personally and those he learned about from others. He probably never went to Colossae, but he joined Epaphras in thanking God and praying for the church in Colossae (Colossians 1:3–14). We don't have to know someone or every detail of a situation to intercede for that person or situation. All we need is the willingness to obey God in helping to fulfill the Great Commission through prayer.

Often the willingness to be obedient is there, but doing it is another matter. Now that we know we are called to intercede, let's pray! First, decide on a specific time each day or week that you will intercede for others throughout the world. I like to go continent-by-continent, or by specific ethnic groups. It is recommended that you write down the various people or world situations that you are praying for. Secondly, before you begin to pray, make sure that there are no unconfessed sins in your life and allow the Holy Spirit to guide you. Finally, fall to your knees and watch how our sovereign God will change the world through prayer.

— ROSLYN YILPET

If we are becoming a world pray-er, like Roslyn, or learning how to pray and be obedient to God's voice concerning our families, God sees our heart, our effort. The greatest lesson and joy for me is knowing I'm joining hands with the divine Prayer Team. If I don't know what to pray about Mali, West Africa, or my grandchild about to be born into a world filled with trouble—I can simply listen to my divine Team, pray, and mimic their prayers. "So, teach the rest of us what to say to God. We are too ignorant to make our own arguments" (Job 37:19 NLT).

— VICTORIA

Listen

God wants to speak to us if we will push the *off* button, and allow our minds and bodies to rest and relax and let His voice enter in. But how do you rest your whole body? I had to practice this for a long time. My mind and body had gotten so used to multitasking even before the phrase became popular. I had to learn how to *actively listen*. Active listening as a communication technique in counseling and conflict resolution requires the listener to repeat to the speaker what she heard, restating or paraphrasing in her own words what the speaker has said. This verifies and confirms the understanding of both parties.

One day I had finished clearing all of the junk in my basement. I then sat down to write. I scribbled down all my ideas for books I would write and all kinds of ministry I would do. As I sat waiting for God's direction, I prayed, *Lord what order do you want these things to fall in? What's first, second, and third?* I was waiting for the Lord to speak to my heart when I heard God say, *Deb, I need you to go rub your husband's back.*

What!? Well, I did intend to obey, but the phone rang (saved by the bell). Then something else happened, followed by something else. Before I knew it, three hours passed. I got into a big argument with my husband and, oh, well, no back rub.

On a different morning, I was on the way to work after praying about something all night. I concluded that I needed to surrender every day and every minute to God's will for my life. It was one of those "I'm yours, Lord" days, like it says in the song by Brenda Lee. I was reaffirming all these declarations on the way to work. Immediately the Holy Spirit detoured me: *Stop at your friend's house.*

What? Stopping at her house is going to make me late for work, I argued. But I could not ignore the request. I had already committed to being all-in that day. So, I rolled up in front of her house. She opened the door like she was expecting me. She even said something like, "I knew you were coming." *What?!* That day she needed a listening ear, someone to be with her, and transportation.

I wonder how many blessings I've missed in my many days of talking to God but not listening to Him. Slowly but surely, I'm learning to shut up! "God speaks in the silence of the heart. Listening is the beginning of prayer," Mother Teresa said.

— DEBRALEE TOWNSEND

I asked Christ into my life as a child. As a teen I read the book, *Rees Howells, Intercessor*, and I accepted his challenge to unconditionally surrender to God. When I turned seventeen, I found myself in the hospital, paralyzed, and in a coma. The medical staff gave my parents very little hope and told them to begin to make my final arrangements. Instead, my parents sent out a call for prayer from all over the world. I'm here today because of those intercessory prayers. God used this experience in my teens, as well as many others, to convince me of the power of prayer.

After college, I started searching for answers to the question, "Why is Christianity not really working in my life and in the lives of God's people?" One of the things I realized from my research is the importance of intercessory prayer. Preaching, teaching, counseling, and addressing the needs of the poor are all good ministry activities. But the ministry of biblically based intercessory prayer is a dynamic tool God put in the hands of His people to accomplish His will in the world.

Once Jesus left this earth, His disciples organized several Christian gatherings, and the main item on the agenda was prayer. It became the very foundation of the New Testament church. And what is said of these twelve men: they "turned the world upside down" (Acts 17:6). Just think about it. Until God calls His children home, Jesus is making intercession for believers. Night and day, 24/7, this is now His main job.

Intercessory prayer is not merely collecting prayer requests and reciting a list before the Lord. Authentic, intercessory prayer—the kind that hits the target every time—has one central element. This kind of prayer asks God His desires. This type of praying is unique and requires intimacy with the Father. The enemy detests this kind of praying and cannot stand against it.

Daniel exemplified this type of praying. When it was time for the captives to return to Israel after their seventy years in Babylon, Daniel just so happened to be reading from Jeremiah's prophecy. He realized the seventy years were up and he prayed, remembering with God His promise (Daniel 9:2).

In the New Testament, another example is Jesus's followers in the upper room. The risen Savior who'd already ascended back to heaven, had told His disciples on several occasions about the coming of the Holy Spirit (John 14, Acts 1:8). I believe those ten days in that room, before the day of Pentecost, were filled with prayer reviewing Jesus's words and promises. One might argue, "Oh, it would have happened anyway because that was God's plan." His Word answers: God is "watching over My word to perform it" (Jeremiah 1:12 NASB).

— REBECCA OSAIGBOVO

Reflect

How can you pray for others and in what contexts is God preparing you to do so?

Think of moments you should have *actively listened*. Are there ways you can practice active listening in your prayer life?

God Knows

My college years are what I call my spiritual vacation. I'd only been a Christian for a few years when I left home, and although Jesus definitely traveled with me, I decided to put my Bible on the shelf and do my own thing. During that time, I became close friends with two people on campus, Perry and Deborah. We hung out together so much that fellow students called us the "Three Musketeers."

Deborah and I graduated, but Perry stayed behind to finish a few more classes. I had rededicated my life to Christ and moved on with my endeavors when I got a phone call from Deborah. "I just found out Perry was killed in a car accident."

I couldn't believe it. Perry was only twenty-something! After I hung up the phone, I sat for a long time thinking and praying. I recalled all the good times the three of us had back in the day. But one devastating thought kept recurring: I could not think of a spiritual conversation I had with Perry over all those years. Oh yeah, I'm sure Deborah and I talked around it; we were both Christians. But at the time, my lifestyle was anything but representing Christ. I never witnessed to Perry or explained the gospel message.

About ten years later, I found myself to be a pastor's wife. I always made it a point to greet visitors. One particular young woman attended sporadically. For some reason, when we greeted each other, the conversation went deeper than hi and bye. I hadn't thought much about Perry and my college experience; however, I kept hearing the phrase, repeating through my mind, *remember Perry.*

One Sunday I stopped her, and we exchanged phone numbers. We arranged for her to come by the parsonage on her lunch break. She poured out her heart to me about her past life of drugs and unhealthy relationships. I was prepared to go through the Scripture about Christianity with her and share the gospel, but after she poured out her story, I hesitated. But then the nagging thought came to me once again, *remember Perry.*

I went through the salvation Scriptures with her, and she emphatically stated, "This is the missing piece. I want Christ to be my Lord and Savior." She prayed a sincere, heartfelt prayer in which she confessed her sinfulness, acknowledged Christ's death on the cross, and expressed her desire for Him. Once she opened her eyes, I had no doubt she understood what had just happened. I gave her some Scriptures to look up and asked her if we could continue to meet. I wanted to help her grow in her newfound faith. She agreed and planned to come the following week at the same time.

I never got that opportunity because she died in a car accident the following week. Instead, at her mother's request, I shared about her newfound Christian commitment at her funeral.

God knew about Perry, and He also knew about the young woman I'd share Christ with years later. He understood the impact both incidents would still have on my life over thirty years later. When I first became a believer, I learned how to explain to a person how to become a believer quickly. I spent more time talking to people about Christ than I spent talking to Christ about people. Everyone needed Jesus, and I had the information in my hands. I had to tell it! I have no doubt that I mowed over several people with my zeal and insensitivity.

Perry, the young woman I shared the gospel with as a pastor's wife, and a few other similar incidents have communicated an enormous message to me. God knows, and we must wait on Him. The Holy Spirit will show you who, how, and when. Psalm 139 is one of my all-time favorite passages. When I pray, I mention it often.

> I will praise thee; for I am fearfully and wonderfully made: marvelous are thy works; and that my soul knoweth right well. My substance was not hid from thee, when I was made in secret, and curiously wrought in the lowest parts of the earth. Thine eyes did see my substance, yet being unperfect; and in thy book all my members were written, which in continuance were fashioned, when as yet there was none of them. How precious also are thy thoughts unto me, O God! how great is the sum of them! (vv. 14–17)

David, the author of the psalm, spoke about God as he knew Him as a brother and as a friend. I've been in the house I live in right now for over twenty-five years. I know my residence from top to bottom. When I get up to go to the bathroom in the dark, I don't need a flashlight because I know exactly how to get there. Now let's take this a step deeper. What if I were the original builder of the home, from digging the foundation to the final touches on the roof? This psalm reminds us that God knit us together in our mother's womb. He's not merely a visitor in the house; instead, He's the original builder.

David also says that every day of our lives is written out in His book. That means that all cells, muscles, bones, skin, and all parts of our body were made by Him and are known to Him. He is aware when our father's sperm hit our mother's egg, and when the embryo started to form. He is entirely aware of the day of our death and knows the details of when it's going to happen, how, and where (v. 16). When I pray with these facts in mind, it causes me to rest. Someone is in charge, and it's not me.

My lifespan is covered by the Almighty; as well He covers my moment-by-moment thoughts. Before a word is spoken out of my mouth, the pre-thought has already been observed by God. He knows all our beliefs, behaviors, and attitudes. Nothing takes Him by surprise. This is an understanding of God that is continuously growing. Someone corrected me when I said something about God's throne room. "You sound like it's a place we have to go to. You realize the throne room is His presence. We are already there." This did help because sometimes I think that I have to get to my quiet place to talk to the Father. It's comforting to know that there's no traveling necessary, and no dialing 911 and waiting. In the good times, difficulties, celebrations, and funerals, He's always there and available to me.

David responded to God by calling His thoughts toward him as "precious" and weighty. He sees them like expensive jewels. Then he goes on to say they are as numerous as sand. It's natural when a problem arises to ask, "How can I fix this? What do I need to do to figure this out? To move forward?" I so appreciate those times when I'm tossing and turning something repeatedly in my mind, and God steps in. Especially at night, when He says, "I got this. I'm already on it, working it out. You go on to sleep."

David's psalm ends with a prayer. I often pray something similar: "God, you know my worries, the places in my heart where I'm not trusting you. Show me where I'm messing up. Lord, lead me like a little lamb. You know I don't know which way to go or how to direct my life."

I traveled with a group of ladies to a women's conference in Michigan. We started out early in the morning leaving from Chicago. A couple of hours into the trip, we got hungry and started asking the driver to look for a place to stop.

One of the mothers on the van instructed the driver to find a rest stop with picnic tables. We had no idea that this mother had a hot meal all prepared and ready to share with us. She had prepared chicken, greens, sweet potatoes, iced tea, and lemon pound cake for dessert. She beamed with pleasure as she laid out this feast before us. She already knew, and she was prepared.

This psalm and my experiences with Perry and the young woman from my church remind me that God already knows. He's prepared to handle what's behind, ahead, and all around us. I used to pray as though I needed to inform God of my circumstances. He does love to hear my voice and spend time with me, but not because He needs my information. He already knows and, like that mother on the van, delights in anticipating my needs and addressing them.

—VICTORIA

Reflect

Describe your intercessory prayer for the people in your life.

Where do you need help and improvement?

Which Scripture or biblical character spoke to your heart?

Blessed
AFTER AMEN

NO LONGER BOUND

I was in a bad relationship with a woman that was much older than me and who brought out the worst in me. I struggled with my connection with God the entire time I was with her. I had no desire to pray.

During the time we were dating, I was a young teen without his father in his life. I felt overwhelmed, angry, and helpless. As a result, I tried to seek comfort in the wrong places. This toxic person seemed to blind me and bind me up. I no longer experienced God's love and I didn't think He cared about me. An older woman at my church, Mary Hinton, helped me to see the light. She told my mother, "I went into prayer for Andre like he was my own son." I believe her prayers pulled me out of this damaging situation. I'll be forever grateful to her.

— CURTIS ANDRE JOHNSON

Somebody Prayed for Me

Growing up, I have vivid memories of "some somebody" praying for me. Those memories make my heart overflow with gratitude, and I sing the song's lyrics "I'm so glad they prayed for me" from "Somebody Prayed for Me," by Dorothy Norwood and Alvin Dorling. Is this type of experience now becoming a rarity among us? Is prayer not as popular a thing to do among emerging generations? Simple practices of saying grace before dinner or prayers before bedtime are no longer standards in many homes. We can see the Judges mindset emerge once again, manifesting all around us: "And also all that generation were gathered unto their fathers: and there arose another generation after them, which knew not the LORD, nor yet the works which he had done for Israel" (Judges 2:10). For many, prayer is seen as an option of the last resort after all else has failed. I suspect that many of the hymns and songs that pulled me through dark nights will be left in archived print and never be sung, or even read again.

As a mom of four and knowing the power of prayer, I model before my children the value of going to God in prayer. Our model at home is praying *first*, no matter what. It is a beautiful thing to see our children live what they are learning. If someone hits their toe or has a fall, we pray first, while seeking first aid if needed. I was in the kitchen preparing dinner and did not realize how hot the pot handle was. I let out a scream, and my three-year-old who has a speech delay ran into the kitchen, and immediately began to pray. All his words were unintelligible, but I knew he was going before God on behalf of my burn.

After he said amen, he asked "Band-Aid?" I smiled and told him I was fine.

Teaching them to pray even in the small things is developing their spirit to pray *first* when life brings the tougher challenges their way. Our thirteen-year-old was hoping for a scholarship to enroll in a private school because we had explained to her that we would not be able to pay for the entire cost. Her response was, "I'll just pray about it." God heard her prayer and provided for her. When we pray, they pray.

We cannot take a passive position in prayer and forget about the coming generations. The evil one is not passive with his assertion that there are alternatives to worship. Therefore, it is crucial that intercessors and prayer warriors stand in the gap to proclaim that before and after the other options have failed, prayer is the answer. Our prayers are invaluable, and generations are depending on them.

> *And you must love the LORD your God with all your heart, all your soul, and all your strength. And you must commit yourselves wholeheartedly to these commands that I am giving you today. Repeat them again and again to your children. Talk about them when you are at home and when you are on the road, when you are going to bed and when you are getting up.* (DEUTERONOMY 6:5–7 NLT)

I believe not only in teaching my children to pray, but teaching any child I meet, and their parents too. I talk about prayer in our home and at every opportunity I have. My heart is to live a life of prayer so that my children and their children may live as well.

— JOLANDA ROGERS

As a child, I would often hear my mother talking to her friends (usually prayer partners and ladies from her Bible study) about "standing in the gap." As often as I heard it, I really did not understand their discussions. When the Pixar animated film *The Incredibles* came out, I saw imagery that really brought this concept to life for me. "Elastigirl" is Mr. Incredible's wife, and her superpower allows her body to stretch in all kinds of ways. In one scene of the movie, there is a considerable gap from one building to the next. To ensure the mission would not fail, Elastigirl extends her body. She plants her feet firmly on one structure, with her torso and arms extending over the gap, and her hands clinging to the other building. The mission was completed successfully.

All of us have a gap somewhere in our lives—a gap between where we are and where we are headed on this journey through life by faith. It may be a gap in faith, a gap in belief, a gap in behavior, a gap in self-love, self-esteem, and self-care. Whatever the hole may be, we members of the body of Christ are bound by one Spirit and one Lord who is in all and through all. As such, when we see where a sister (or brother) is present, and we see where they are headed, but we also see the struggles, the failures, the frustrations, the doubt, we must build them up (Jude 1:20–23). That is the time when we are called to intercede on their behalf—to stand in the gap between where they are and where they are going. We are called to be a sort of spiritual Elastigirl.

How much more powerful would we be as a body of Christ, if, when we saw our sister struggling, we prayed. Spending some time before the Father on her behalf rather than critically pondering, *why is this situation such an issue for her? Why can't she seem to get it together, or why does she always get trapped in the same predicament?* We pray for her strength to overcome. We pray for her self-esteem, and we trust in God to believe she can. We pray for God's power to be realized in her life. We pray against the forces of the enemy that seem always to know just the right time to attack her. We pray against deceptions that might be present. We pray. We bridge the gap between her current reality and what is to come.

In the Gospels, we find friends who stood in the gap for their beloved brother who was physically paralyzed (Mark 2:1–12). They knew where Jesus was, and they knew that Jesus had the power to heal. They overcame the obstacle of the crowd and the roof to put their friend at Jesus's feet for His healing. They stood in the gap. Sometimes we encounter people who are emotionally and spiritually paralyzed. They can't bring themselves to Jesus for healing. But like the friends in the book of Mark and the character Elastigirl, we can bridge the gap between where they are and where they are going through our faith, through our prayers, and through our actions. Standing in the gap is not passive. It's tenacious. It's aggressive. It's no holds barred. It's pressing and fighting for the future of others in Christ Jesus.

The next time someone's actions rub us the wrong way, we can ask the Lord to reveal to us their need. Then stretch our faith across the gap of where they are and where God is calling them to be. This way, God gets the glory and the body of Christ is edified.

— YULISE WATERS

Reflection

Who are you standing in the gap for?

Let Us Pray

As we intercede with Christ for others, this section provides some rallying points.

PRAYING FOR YOUTH

The youth group director at my church, Mrs. Towns, offered me a job as a teaching assistant at the school where she served as principal. She observed my speaking gift and deep compassion for the children. I finished my last two years of high school as a correspondence student, so I was available during the day. I accepted Mrs. Towns's offer, and she began to train me. I was only sixteen, but my heart went out to the youth, especially the boys coming from fatherless homes. They always seemed so confused and lost.

Now, almost twenty years later, I'm still teaching, and my soul remains committed to children attending inner-city schools; the boys my primary concern. African American and Latino males make up most of the prison system in the United States. If they're not incarcerated, so many get lost or die (physically or emotionally) along the way.

I'm always challenging Christians to pray for the students I work with, but especially the young males. I see them as future leaders in their homes and our communities, and envision them as young, future kings.

—CANDACEE JOHNSON

Children raised without a father in the home is a problem.

If the male child is raised by uncles, grandfathers, older brothers, or other male figures this is helpful; however, that's if the person is an excellent example with a confident voice. But if those men are drug dealers, abusive, lazy, and not walking in God's purpose, it hurts the boys. The boys need affirmative role models. They need men who are willing to come into the schools, tell their stories, and teach young children about their real-life journeys. They need to be shown how to be fathers and husbands, and how to raise and lead a family. Men who walk in genuineness, integrity, and courage.

Pray for a resolution of anger issues. So many children are subjected to trauma and abuse, which all too often causes them to do the same to others. Anger results in trouble at school, fights, and being disrespectful to the adults who are trying to help them. But a person subjected to past hurts has unprocessed trauma, which results in triggers. Anyone who sets off one of these personal alarms that is connected to submerged feelings receives the person's anger. The people closest to them get the brunt of their pain and frustration.

Too many young males are placed in detention, are suspended, or decide to drop out of school. This not only perpetuates spending more time removed from learning in the classroom, but it also gets them in a mindset for a life of displacement, as well as loneliness. We need more time during the school days devoted to teaching young men how to process through their issues, cope with anger, and understand the consequences of criminal behavior. Also, provide opportunities for them to express themselves.

Pray for them to have positive male role models; the dominant figures in the home and the community are often mothers, aunties, or other female relatives or friends. They are not getting an understanding of what a man should be. This causes many of our young men to be confused about their identity.

Pray for the ending of generational curses. Whenever I have conversations with young men about their behavior choices, I always ask them about their fathers and grandfathers. Many times, their decisions are similar to those made by their fathers and grandfathers. This is not only reflected by their outward behavior, but it's an internal, spiritual battle within their souls. I help them understand that through their relationship with Jesus Christ and the power of the Holy Spirit, the curse will and can be broken!

Pray for the strength to resist peer pressure. Young men are faced every day with the choice to be a leader or a follower. Standing alone is often very difficult for many young men, but it's especially hard when they have been abandoned by their family or society. Our young men strongly desire and need a place to belong and to feel accepted. Peers offer this refuge, either positively or negatively. On social media, they have created terms and contexts that seem to offer some belonging but, in fact, do not.

Pray for them to get a personal vision and understand their purpose. Without vision, people perish (Proverbs 29:18). A young man without dreams is a sad young man. If he walks around unaware of his God-given purpose, and without knowledge about his mission in life, that's a recipe for disaster.

Because then others will begin to define his future. When I asked a group of young men, "What do you want to be when you grow up?" Many of them responded that they want to be a sports player or just make a lot of money. I wonder if they are concerned about living and dying. It's very rare to hear, "I want to be a doctor or an engineer." This is due not only to a lack of exposure to these different possibilities but also due to a lack of belief in their own capabilities. Many are potential teachers, preachers, scientists, mathematicians, and many other great professions. But they question, "How do I get there? I've never met anyone in these positions." There is a need for men in these occupations to speak to the boys in the schools and community centers. The men must not come in just suited and booted, but they must be prepared to share the ups and downs of their journeys honestly. They must share what it takes to get and keep a good paying job, own your own business, have a healthy, beautiful family, and how to get out of the "hood."

Pray for the spirit of mourning and death to be lifted. Many young men have lost their fathers or someone close to them (like a grandparent who raised them) through murders, shootings, health issues, or suicide, perhaps because of struggles with their mental health. Many young men have seen death and bloodshed in front of them. They have been to funerals and seen their family members and friends in coffins. Some have even seen family members or friends holding the bodies of their relatives or friends who have died at the hands of violence. No doubt, some of these young men need counseling after such trauma. Sadly, family, schools, and churches may be uninformed or lack resources to help.

This spirit of death and sadness can also be brought into their lives in the form of verbal, sexual, or physical abuse. Many of the boys have been abused so severely by a guardian, former teacher, or group of friends that they lack confidence. Their lives are overshadowed by low self-esteem, shame, and hurt. Many of them have never been able to tell their stories and express their hurt and pain in a safe environment or with someone they trust. Authorities who were supposed to protect them have hurt them.

They deal with it the best way they know how, which comes out either through abuse of others, through addictions, or anger. Masking the pain and never healing, they take this pain to their families and carry on the unhealthy tradition.

Pray that they will be able to receive God's truth about themselves rather than the lies of the enemy. Some of these young males have endured cursing, been called out of their names, and been spoken to negatively from day one. Eventually, those things become what they believe about themselves. I pray that more Christians will build them up and let them know who they are in Christ, and speak life to them, rather than continue the messages of death. They need to be encouraged to talk positively to their peers rather than bullying or taking them down. I continually say, "Lift your head high, you are a young king." It's incredible to see the empowering results when a young man is told affirmations about himself.

— VICTORIA

PRAYING FOR THE INCARCERATED

When I went into court with my son who was in trouble with the criminal justice system, I used to pray for everybody in the courtroom. That included everyone from the judge to the officer at the back door. I prayed for his whole situation to be turned around, and for my son to come home. I still pray those kinds of prayers, but there is one that has now taken precedence over all the rest. I pray for my son to surrender to God entirely.

He's had a lot of time to think about what he's going to do when he gets out. This includes the contacts he plans to make, people he's going to see, and his plans to be vocal about the injustices he and others have endured. While this is all good, I try to help him understand that it's all fruitless unless God is in the lead. I tell him, "If you are just doing things on your own, it's not going to work." In fact, living independently of God and refusing to listen to the Holy Spirit's direction is imprisonment within.

I want my son to come home, and we all miss him terribly. But I also want him to be free, inside and out.

— DEBRALEE TOWNSEND

PRAYER FOR CHURCHES

When people ask how my prayer ministry started, I must admit, it started with me in my basement, when I asked the Lord to make himself real to me. As a believer, I needed to comprehend God operating in my situation as I was experiencing needs in my marriage and family. I prayed and came upstairs a very different person.

God began to reveal himself to me in my prayer times and they became even more meaningful. I not only could see His answers to my prayers, but also God began to show me others in need of prayer. More than thirty years ago now, God started my prayer ministry in my church. We meet at 6:00 a.m. Saturday mornings. From the seniors who've been walking with the Lord a long time, to "babies in Christ" — we've seen so many answers to prayer: we've witnessed healings, jobs obtained, marriages restored, criminal cases resolved.

It's a blessing to be a part of this ministry and I pray the generations realize their prayer power as we invest the time, given the promise: "Now all glory to God, who is able, through his mighty power at work within us, to accomplish infinitely more than we might ask or think. Glory to him in the church and in Christ Jesus through all generations forever and ever! Amen (Ephesians 3:20–21 NLT).

— NAOMI BROWN

Reflect

How have you seen yourself as someone who prays for men? Father, brother, husband, or son?

How have you been guilty of misjudging, and how can you call on God to help you to change in this area?

Write out a brief prayer concerning an African American man or group of men who need your intercession.

Journaling Our Praise

After our amen, God is still praying, and encouraging us to keep on praying. Many years ago, I wrote Jordan's name in my praise and prayer journal, along with Colossians 1:9–28 and John 15:5–11. Whenever I would meet Jordan, I would ask, "How are you doing?" He always provided the same reply, "I could be better." The Holy Spirit within me would always cringe because Jordan's reply seemed to indicate his lack of knowing Jesus's love and contentment. I specifically prayed for Jordan not only to come to know Jesus, but for him to grow in Christ, to bear fruit, and experience God's joy.

After ten years of praying this specific prayer for Jordan, my family visited him. Jordan enthusiastically shared with us that he had not only received Jesus Christ but had begun growing spiritually through Bible Study Fellowship. He is now a leader who teaches others. God chose to answer my ten years of prayers for Jordan "more than all we ask or imagine" (Ephesians 3:20 NIV).

After almost twenty years of praying for the Wilson family, my prayers haven't been fully answered. I specifically wrote down each family member's name. I pray weekly that they will walk according to God's will in their lives (see Ephesians 4:1–2). Recently, I visited the parents, who updated me on each of their children's lives, including their spiritual walk with God. I continue to pray for the family, using specific Scripture as the Holy Spirit leads.

I have been journaling in one form or another since my youth. Some respond to the suggestion of journaling with no resistance, "It will be easy." Other people, however, react, "I hate journaling and have never been consistent with it. It won't work for me!" Whatever our stance, scriptural praise and prayer journaling can transform our intercessory prayer life. What is scriptural praise-prayer journaling? We systematically write specific praises and prayer requests (a journal or notebook works well with regular use during praise and prayer time). The emphasis is a written document as a guideline.

Praise-prayer journaling is unique because we use specific Scriptures, given through the guidance of the Holy Spirit, for each praise and prayer request. God's Word has power. "For the word of God is alive and active. Sharper than any double-edged sword, it penetrates even to dividing soul and spirit, joints and marrow; it judges the thoughts and attitudes of the heart" (Hebrews 4:12 NIV). Using Scripture to praise God glorifies Him by agreeing with what He has already said to be true about himself. Praying specific Scripture verses for others and ourselves releases God's power to work in our lives according to His will:

> *This is the confidence we have in approaching God: that if we ask anything according to his will, he hears us. And if we know that he hears us—whatever we ask—we know that we have what we asked of him.*
> (1 JOHN 5:14–15 NIV)

Praying God's will to Him assures us that He will answer our prayers in His timing.

Why keep a journal of praise and prayer requests? Our minds are forgetful. Writing our praises and prayer requests helps us to remember God's character as well as the specific needs of others. Using a scriptural praise-prayer journal testifies what God has done in our lives and strengthens our faith and others'. First Chronicles 16:12 instructs us to "Remember the wonders that he has done." Starting and implementing a praise and prayer journal helps us to fulfill this instruction.

How to begin and implement a scriptural praise-prayer journal? Your journal can be handmade or purchased, organized by topics, days, or both. I prefer to use both. My journal is divided by the days of the week, and each day has a specific topic. For example, on Sunday, I praise God for the body of Christ and pray specifically for various churches. On Wednesday, I pray for foreign missions and the world. Other prayer topics include those who need salvation, family and friends, coworkers, and groups that I have interacted with over the years. Each request is prayed for using one or more Scripture verses as the Spirit leads.

Implementing your journal is the key to transforming your intercessory prayer life. You will be amazed at how your time with God is enriched and empowered as you daily praise Him and pray for others using Scripture. Remember to write down when and how God answers your requests explicitly. For example, one time I was praying for God to provide a specific home for us. I referenced Philippians 4:19, that God will meet my needs. God answered that prayer, but not with that home. A scriptural praise-prayer journal is a useful tool to enrich our fellowship with God.

— ROSLYN YILPET

When we enter into God's family, we are given countless spiritual blessings in Christ. We are chosen by God, considered royal, holy, blameless, adopted, accepted, forgiven, able to access divine wisdom, and live with the hope of an eternal home (see 1 Peter 2:9; Ephesians 1:1–14). This only begins to scratch the surface of all that the Father wants to give us now, and throughout eternity.

Devote yourselves to prayer, being watchful and thankful. (COLOSSIANS 4:2 NIV)

Pray in the Spirit at all times and on every occasion. Stay alert and be persistent in your prayers for all believers everywhere. (EPHESIANS 6:18 NLT)

Contributors

Cynthia A. Atkins enjoys women's advocacy. She is a business entrepreneur and a pastor of Zion Family Worship Center in New Jersey. She's an adjunct professor at New Jersey City University, and recipient of the Union County Women of Excellence Award for Women's Advocacy. Dr. Atkins is also an author of two books, *Revealed Intercession* and *Dream Mapping*. Passionate about prayer, she organizes prayer and Bible study in the Union County Division of Social Service.

Breonna Rostic is a wife, mother, and mentor engaging in youth and prayer ministry through hands-on work in her local church and community in Grand Rapids, Michigan. She's passionate about creating biblical content to reach millennial women, teaching them the hope of the gospel, the truth about transformation, and purpose. Breonna is a breakout writer and speaker featured in *Our Daily Bread*; *Our Help: Devotions on Struggle, Victory, Legacy*; YMI; and *Relevant*.

JoLanda Rogers shares messages of healing, hope, and survival. She is a wife and mother and the founder of T.A.L.K. Consulting, LLC, where she encourages others as a professional counselor and caregiver. A survivor and advocate for victims of gender-based violence, JoLanda has published a series for survivors of childhood sexual abuse. She is a contributing writer at *Our Daily Bread*.

Joyce M. Dinkins is a wife and mother who has also experienced single parenting. She enjoys speaking, writing, reading, and traveling to share God's love. Joyce is executive editor of Our Daily Bread Ministries Voices Collection, and serves at Emmanuel Community Church, South Haven, Michigan. She is a member of the Academy of Christian Editors and loves to encourage.

Antone Hays is a mother, grandmother, and great-grandmother who enjoys playing the piano, singing hymns, and gardening. She loves serving in the music ministry at New Testament Church, Milwaukee, Wisconsin; mentoring; and telling others about Christ. She led many coworkers and clients to the Lord as a social service employee.

Constance Alberts is a wife, mother, and grandmother who enjoys collecting candles and decorating. She has served at Riverwest Community Church in Milwaukee, Wisconsin, for more than twenty years and is Sunday school superintendent. The first college graduate in her family, she's employed by the Urban Economic Development Association as financial capability project manager to promote financial literacy and empowerment.

Georgia Hill has pursued missions in Detroit, Michigan; Mexico; Tanzania; South Africa; Liberia; and Panama. She is Associate Pastor of Plymouth United Church of Christ, serves on the Harper Hutzel Hospital Ethics Committee, is a member of the Plymouth Housing Board, and teaches at Wayne State University in the African American Studies Department. She conducts women's Bible studies, hosts a women's telephone prayer line, and leads Revelation Dance Ministry. A licensed attorney, she practiced law for several years before working in city government.

Mother Adell B. Dickerson is a wife, mother, and grandmother who delights in loving God and serving people as a certified biblical counselor, intercessor, Bible teacher, and freelance writer. She is a contributor to the *Wisdom and Grace Devotional Bible,* and is an author of leadership training materials. She serves as the International Supervisor of Women, New Pentecostal Church, Inc., and leads a Bible Study Fellowship (BSF) group.

Tina Payne is a wife, mother, and grandmother who enjoys traveling, entertaining, gardening, and attending inspirational movies about beating the odds. She's passionate about and praying to see reconciliation in her community in Milwaukee, Wisconsin, as well as across the globe. Tina is an advocate for National Alliance for Mental Illness (NAMI), helps the disadvantaged, and desires justice for all.

Michelle R. Loyd-Paige is a wife, mother, and grandmother, and a strong advocate for living a balanced life with time for rest, play, and good food. Executive associate to the president for diversity and inclusion at Calvin University in Western

Michigan, Michelle is also associate pastor of Angel Community Church; founder and CEO of PreachSista! Inc., a nonprofit organization encouraging women in ministry; and the founder of Loyd Paige & Associates diversity consulting.

Ericka Loynes is a wife and mother who encourages others through career coaching, motivational speaking, and inspirational writing. A senior instructional designer and facilitator for a national retail company, Ericka has also written devotionals for *Words of Hope*, *Our Daily Bread*, and is a contributing writer to *Guideposts* magazine.

Cokiesha Bailey Robinson is married, and a missionary who has traveled throughout the United States, and to Africa, Jamaica, and Turkey. Previously on staff as director of growth at Concord Church, Dallas, Texas, she was also assistant pastor of Mt. Neboh Church, New York, New York. She has coauthored two books, contributed to eight more, and now contributes to *Our Daily Bread*. She is a full-time itinerant minister of the gospel and founder of Cross Spring Ministries.

Yulise R. Waters is a wife, mother, and the director of Dallas Programs for Lone Star Justice Alliance. She oversees the programmatic, data, development, and community engagement aspects of the Second Chance Community Improvement Program (SCCIP), the first-ever alternative to incarceration for young adults in Texas. Waters is passionate about people living the abundant life God has for us.

Maria A. Westbrook is married and co-ministers with her husband at the church they founded, Greater Life Christian Fellowship Church, Philadelphia. Maria is an anointed gospel singer and loves writing sermons and workshops on the importance of prayer and healing. She is also a professional grant writer and contributing author of *African American Church Leadership, Elijah's Mantle*, and *Our Help: Devotions on Struggle, Victory, Legacy*. She serves several collaborative efforts and boards, including the Summit Group for Black Family Development.

Lydia Turner is married and became the mother of her first child at this writing. She enjoys bargain hunting and adding her artistic flair to any number of projects. Her personal mission is to help build God's kingdom through her gifts and talents in art, teaching, counseling, and training. She is a licensed professional counselor, registered art therapist, and a spiritual director for individuals, couples, families, and groups.

J. Wright enjoys spending quality time with family and friends and watching movies. She owns her own business in Milwaukee, Wisconsin. As a "purpose coach," she helps women entrepreneurs visualize, organize, and make plans to move forward their business ideas.

Sandra Foster is a wife, mother, and grandmother who loves taking time to pray, visit the sick, and bargain hunt. Sincerely devoted to her church, Solomon's Temple Evangelistic Ministries in Milwaukee, Wisconsin, Sandra serves as the head intercessor. She also belongs to a community Christian group that meets each morning to pray for local and global requests.

Sharon Norris Elliott is a wife, mother, and grandmother. Her inspiring message as a licensed minister, Bible teacher, award-winning author, and popular conference speaker is "Live significantly!" Author of eleven books, Sharon is also a professional editor and writing coach. Her TV show, *Life That Matters,* broadcasts online.

Mary Smith is a wife, mother, grandmother, and great-grand-mother who grew up living next door to her future husband and ministry partner. Together they do couples ministry where they live in Milwaukee, Wisconsin. Their desire is to lead young men and women to Christ. They are committed to the intercessory prayer ministry in their church, New Testament, and also organize ways for people to pray for requests through-out the local community and nation.

Renee Williams Logbo is a wife and mother who loves to sew, work in real estate, and sing. In her compassion to help chil-dren, she has welcomed eighty-nine to stay at her home. She adopted three. Renee is president of the choir at Progressive Baptist Church in Milwaukee, Wisconsin.

Kimberly Townsend is a mother with a heart for helping oth-ers. She combines her creativity and business savvy to help people and has been on several mission trips in the United

States and overseas. She is the owner of Christian Victory Coach, Oxygen H2O, and author of *Teach Me How to Swaddle* and *Respect Yourself: You're the Daughter of the King*. She is a certified lay minister in counseling and a certified nurse assistant.

Juliette Allen is a wife, mother, and grandmother who enjoys crafting, word games, and baking. She is a Christian education leader at Jubilee Baptist Church, Bartlett, Illinois. She's a board member of AALR and Liberia Life Ministries. Juliet owns Legacy Keepsake Creations. She is a contributor to *Our Help: Devotions on Struggle, Victory, Legacy* and *Unapologetically Woman*.

Diane Proctor Reeder is a widow, mother, and grandmother. This Detroit-based author, playwright, and editor has worked with numerous Christian authors, motivational speakers, and artists. Her latest book is *What the Word BE: Why Black English is the King's (James) English*. She has contributed to several writings: *The Inspiring Grandmother; Our Help: Devotionals on Struggle, Victory, Legacy;* and several *Our Daily Bread* devotionals.

Karynthia Glasper-Phillips is a wife who enjoys crocheting, horseback riding, painting, and playing the flute. She has a passion for a revival of Scripture reading. A bi-vocational minister and medical practitioner, she is an adjunct professor at American Baptist College. In her workshops, coaching, and blogs, she integrates the importance of self-care of spirit, mind, and body. She is a contributing author in Bishop Vashti M. McKenzie's book, *Not Without a Struggle: Leadership for African American Women in Ministry.* She lives and works in Nashville, Tennessee.

Mother Clotea Ware started her spiritual journey as a Sunday school teacher and then began attending Detroit Bible College. She was a pastor's wife for 42 years, ministering alongside her husband. She presently teaches women's Bible studies and adult Sunday school classes. She is also a praise team singer, teaches at a nursing home, and has participated with the Boys and Girls Bible Club in various capacities for more than 50 years. She leads the prayer ministry for the United Conference for Women and has several daily prayer partners. At the age of 86, she continues to call and pray with the elderly and at all-night prayers.

Debralee Townsend is a wife, mother, and grandmother living in Joliet, Illinois. Self-employed as an anger-management consultant and presenter with numerous certifications, she has created initiatives for positive youth activity, and founded and directs "Hygiene Bank," to increase school attendance and performance. She has written *Clean Your Room* and coauthored *101 Anger Management Exercises* and *The Best Purpose-Driven Anger Management Workbook Ever.*

Roslyn R. Yilpet loves teaching and traveling. As a youth growing up in Detroit, she made a dramatic decision that led to her fulfilling both passions. She ventured to Jos, Nigeria, West Africa, forty years ago as a missionary teacher. She is the director of Open Doors for Special Learners in Jos, freelance writes Sunday school lessons, and has written several articles on marriage, family life, and learning disabilities in Nigeria.

Rebecca Osaigbovo is a wife, mother, and grandmother originally from Tennessee. Raised in a missionary family, she now resides in Ypsilanti, Michigan. She recently retired from the nursing profession. Her first book was *Chosen Vessels: Women of Color, Keys to Change.* Her other books include *Movin' on Up, It's Not About You,* and *Spiritual Sisterhood.* Her speaking ministry has taken her across the United States, Canada, Uganda, and Ethiopia.

Candacee Johnson loves spending her free time having fun with her nephew, along with swimming and roller-skating. She began evangelizing as an elementary school child in her neighborhood. By sixteen, she was a teaching assistant in a Christian school. Since graduating from the University of Wisconsin, Milwaukee, she has directed several summer and afterschool programs. As a motivational speaker, she has challenged professional women at a conference in Ethiopia.

Naomi Brown is a wife, mother, and grandmother who stands on this verse: "The LORD hath heard my supplication; the LORD will receive my prayer" (Psalm 6:9). A licensed minister, Naomi is a faithful, active member of Mt. Zion Baptist Church where she spearheads the intercessory prayer ministry, encouraging others to "pray until something happens."

And, thank you to my son:

Curtis Andre Johnson is a father, and a counselor at Bay View High School and believes mentoring youth is his gift from God. He enjoys modeling, and has traveled to Paris to model for Fashion Week. He's definitely smiling when he's playing a good game of basketball, watching sports, or holding his sleeping son on his lap.

— VICTORIA

Acknowledgments

Joyce Dinkins, I still remember the day you said, "I think you should write a book on prayer." I thought: *a book on prayer is nowhere on my list of books I want to write before I die. Where is she getting this?*

Thank you, Lord, and thank you, Joyce. I needed to write this book. It's been spiritually transforming. Thank you, Joyce, for listening to Him and encouraging me to carry out this project. Your prayers, editing, and input have been invaluable. Thank you, Discovery House and Our Daily Bread Ministries, for believing in me. And thank you, Matthew Parker, for having the vision for bringing us all together. Your vision and leadership have helped to advance the ministry of many of us.

A special thanks to my husband, David, for your patience with me as I've spent all this time poring over this project. And praise God for my three children, Lydia, Candacee, and Andre. You are always my cheerleaders and always honest with me about everything. Thank you, Ma, Mattie Saunders, and my extended family for being there for me.

I also need to thank my spiritual moms and sisters, who pray for me more than I know. I'm not going to start listing names because I'm sure to miss somebody, and you know who you are.

I've got to give a shout out to my prayer groups who've interceded faithfully for this book: the 6:00 a.m. Eastbrook Church group, the Wednesday noon and evening Progressive Baptist Church group, and the Wednesday all-day prayer group at New Testament Church, all in Milwaukee.

Thank you for the team of editors and readers, those in Milwaukee and elsewhere. You helped clean up and evaluate this manuscript. Lord knows I needed every last one of you.

And a big thank-you to all the contributors. There is a richness and an anointing in this book because of each of you. Thank you for being open and vulnerable with your stories.

And last, but definitely not least, thank you, Jesus, my Lord and Savior, who has been my precious Shepherd, leading me into beautiful places to get to know a mighty God and to do a work for His kingdom. You keep making Ephesians 3:20 a reality in my life: "Now all glory to God, who is able, through his mighty power at work within us, to accomplish infinitely more than we might ask or think" (NLT).

About the Author

VICTORIA SAUNDERS MCAFEE is an internationally recognized writer and speaker with a passion for women's Bible study and serving others who suffer with sexual abuse issues and emotional pain. She has served at Campus Crusade for Christ, at a crisis pregnancy resource center as an assistant director, and at Moody Bible Institute as an extension instructor. Victoria's books include *The Sister's Guide to In-Depth Bible Study* and *Restoring Broken Vessels*. She's also been a feature writer in *Our Daily Bread*. Victoria resides in Milwaukee, Wisconsin, with her husband, David.

More great books from the Our Daily Bread Voices Collection

<<

Our Help

From a mosaic of multigenerational authors, this inspiring devotional collection reminds us of the hope we have in Christ.

>>

A Voice as Soft as a Honey Bee's Flutter

Journey with Junior as he learns to listen for the voice of God. Young readers and their grown-ups experience the wisdom of Psalm 46 through a colorful masterpiece by award-winning author and illustrator **Jan Spivey Gilchrist.**

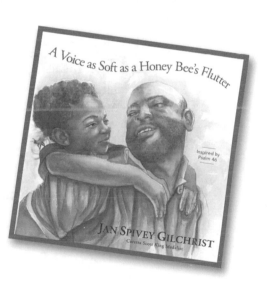

ourdailybreadpublishing.org

FREE RESOURCE

This Far By Faith

This special edition of *Our Daily Bread* celebrates God's faithfulness seen in the heritage of the Black Church.

To order visit odb.org

Help us get the word out!

Our Daily Bread Publishing exists to feed the soul with the Word of God.

If you appreciated this book, please let others know.

- Pick up another copy to give as a gift.
- Share a link to the book or mention it on social media.
- Write a review on your blog, on a bookseller's website, or at our own site (ourdailybreadpublishing.org).
- Recommend this book for your church, book club, or small group.

Connect with us:

 @ourdailybread

 @ourdailybread

 @ourdailybread

Our Daily Bread Publishing
PO Box 3566
Grand Rapids, Michigan 49501 USA

 books@odb.org